DiDA

Unit 1: Using ICT

MARTIN BARRALL & DAVE PARRY

Hodder Arnold

A MEMBER OF THE HODDER HEADLINE GROUP

Orders: please contact Bookpoint Ltd, 130 Milton Park, Abingdon, Oxon OX14 4SB. Telephone: (44) 01235 827720. Fax: (44) 01235 400454. Lines are open from 9.00 to 5.00, Monday to Saturday, with a 24-hour message answering service. You can also order through our website www.hoddereducation.co.uk

If you have any comments to make about this, or any of our other titles, please send them to educationenquiries@hodder.co.uk

British Library Cataloguing in Publication Data
A catalogue record for this title is available from the British Library

ISBN-10: 0 340 915 293
ISBN-13: 978 0 340 915 295

First Edition Published 2006
Impression number 10 9 8 7 6 5 4 3 2 1
Year 2011 2010 2009 2008 2007 2006

This high quality material is endorsed by Edexcel and has been through a rigorous quality assurance programme to ensure that it is a suitable companion to the specification for both learners and teachers. This does not mean that its contents will be used verbatim when setting examinations nor is it to be read as being the official specification – a copy of which is available at www.edexcel.org.uk

Typeset by Pantek Arts Ltd, Maidstone, Kent.
Printed in Great Britain for Hodder Arnold, an imprint of Hodder Education, a member of the Hodder Headline Group, 338 Euston Road, London NW1 3BH

ELECTRONIC END USER SINGLE USE LICENCE AGREEMENT

FOR **DiDA Unit 1: Using ICT CD-ROM Student Version** software published by Hodder and Stoughton Limited (HS) under its Hodder Arnold imprint.

NOTICE TO USER:
THIS IS A CONTRACT. BY INSTALLING THIS SOFTWARE YOU AND OTHERS TO WHOM YOU ALLOW ACCESS TO THE SOFTWARE ACCEPT ALL THE TERMS AND CONDITIONS OF THIS AGREEMENT.

This End User Single Use Licence Agreement accompanies the **DiDA Unit 1: Using ICT CD-ROM Student Version** software (the Software) and shall also apply to any upgrades, modified versions or updates of the Software licensed to you by HS. Please read this Agreement carefully. Upon installing this software you will be asked to accept this Agreement and continue to install or, if you do not wish to accept this Agreement, to decline this Agreement, in which case you will not be able to use the Software.

Upon your acceptance of this Agreement, HS grants to you a non-exclusive, non-transferable licence to install, run and use the Software, subject to the following:

1. Use of the Software. **You may only install a single copy of the Software onto the hard disk or other storage device of only one computer**. If the computer is linked to a local area network then it must be installed in such a way so that the Software cannot be accessed by other computers on the same network. You may make a single back-up copy of the Software (which must be deleted or destroyed on expiry or termination of this Agreement). Except for that single back-up copy, you may not make or distribute any copies of the Software, or use it in any way not specified in this Agreement.

2. Copyright. The Software is owned by HS and its authors and suppliers, and is protected by Copyright Law. Except as stated above, this Agreement does not grant you any intellectual property rights in the Software or in the contents of **DiDA Unit 1: Using ICT CD-ROM** as sold. All moral rights of artists and all other contributors to the Software are hereby asserted.

3. Restrictions. You assume full responsibility for the use of the Software and agree to use the Software legally and responsibly. You agree that you or any other person within or acting on behalf of the purchasing institution shall NOT: use or copy the Software otherwise than as specified in clause 1; transfer, distribute, rent, loan, lease, sub-lease or otherwise deal in the Software or any part of it; alter, adapt, merge, modify or translate the whole or any part of the Software for any purpose; or permit the whole or any part of the Software to be combined with or incorporated in any other product or program. You agree not to reverse engineer, decompile, disassemble or otherwise attempt to discover the source code of the Software. You may not alter or modify the installer program or any other part of the Software or create a new installer for the Software.

4. No Warranty. The Software is being delivered to you AS IS and HS makes no warranty as to its use or performance except that the Software will perform substantially as specified. HS AND ITS AUTHORS AND SUPPLIERS DO NOT AND CANNOT GIVE ANY WARRANTY REGARDING THE PERFORMANCE OR RESULTS YOU MAY OBTAIN BY USING THE SOFTWARE OR ACCOMPANYING OR DERIVED DOCUMENTATION. HS AND ITS AUTHORS AND SUPPLIERS MAKE NO WARRANTIES, EXPRESS OR IMPLIED, AS TO NON-INFRINGEMENT OF THIRD PARTY RIGHTS, THE CONTENT OF THE SOFTWARE, MERCHANTABILITY, OR FITNESS FOR ANY PARTICULAR PURPOSE. IN NO EVENT WILL HS OR ITS AUTHORS OR SUPPLIERS BE LIABLE TO YOU FOR ANY CONSEQUENTIAL, INCIDENTAL, SPECIAL OR OTHER DAMAGES, OR FOR ANY CLAIM BY ANY THIRD PARTY (INCLUDING PERSONS WITH WHOM YOU HAVE USED THE SOFTWARE TO PROVIDE LEARNING SUPPORT) ARISING OUT OF YOUR INSTALLATION OR USE OF THE SOFTWARE.

5. Entire liability. HS's entire liability, and your sole remedy for a breach of the warranty given under Clause 4, is (a) the replacement of the Software not meeting the above limited warranty and which is returned by you within 90 days of purchase; or (b) if HS or its distributors are unable to deliver a replacement copy of the Software you may terminate this Agreement by returning the Software within 90 days of purchase and your money will be refunded. All other liabilities of HS including, without limitation, indirect, consequential and economic loss and loss of profits, together with all warranties, are hereby excluded to the fullest extent permitted by law.

6. Governing Law and General Provisions. This Agreement shall be governed by the laws of England and any actions arising shall be brought before the courts of England. If any part of this Agreement is found void and unenforceable, it will not affect the validity of the balance of the Agreement, which shall remain wholly valid and enforceable according to its terms. All rights not specifically licensed to you under this Agreement are reserved to HS. This Agreement shall automatically terminate upon failure by you to comply with its terms. This Agreement is the entire and only agreement between the parties relating to its subject matter. It supersedes any and all previous agreements and understandings (whether written or oral) relating to its subject matter and may only be amended in writing, signed on behalf of both parties.

Using ICT Student's CD-ROM

The enclosed single-user licence CD-ROM contains various resources designed to assist your throughout your course. The CD-ROM has several features, including sections that correspond to the chapters in this textbook. These features include:

- Exercises: there are one or two exercises in this section for each chapter of the textbook. Each one will help you to consolidate your knowledge of a particular topic. Some require you to refer to a specific website, for others there are associated files that you can use to complete the exercise. Whenever associated files are mentioned in an exercise they are written in CAPITALS and a link to the file itself will appear in the 'Resource File' panel on the right hand side of the page.
- Tutorials: These demonstrations of how to use various software packages are available in those chapters (12-19) that relate directly to software applications. Short descriptions of each skill will appear when you roll the mouse pointer over each tutorial link.
- Useful links: this section contains useful links to other websites and resources relevant to each particular topic. If you are connected to the internet, simply clicking on each link will open the website in a new web browser window. Please note: All weblinks contain live content and information, and as such this content is liable to change. Hodder & Stoughton Ltd are not responsible for the content of any external website. An assessment of the appropriateness of each website for the intended audience should be undertaken by a responsible adult
- Resource bank: This area provides a range of dummy files for you to practice your software skills on. They are nothing more than examples of each type of file, to help you to get used to the sorts of files you will be working with when studying DiDA Unit 1. You can take each file and do whatever you want with it – stretch it, squash it, edit it, delete it…! Some of these files are duplicates of those that are used in exercises from the student and teacher sections; other files only appear in this section.

Before you start using this CD ROM, it may be helpful to refer to the 'How to use this CD-ROM' section, which you can access from the main menu screen. Included in this area is a tutorial that will provide you with a step-by-step introduction to accessing and using the different types of resources available on this CD-ROM.

Contents

Acknowledgements

The authors would like to thank Drew Buddie for all his help in preparing the manuscript for publication.

Every effort has been made to trace and acknowledge ownership of copyright. The publishers will be glad to make suitable arrangements with any copyright holders whom it has not been possible to contact.
The author and publishers would like to thank the following for the use of photographs in this volume:

Stock4b Gmbh/Photolibrary **px**; Mark Hodson LRPS/ www.hodsonphoto.com/photographersdirect.com **p6**; Digital Focus/ Alamy **p8**; Lightworks Media/ Alamy **p10**; Ace Stock Ltd/ Alamy **p10**; Workbook, Inc/ Photolibrary **p23** (top); Steve Blogg/ Rex Features **p23** (bottom); Photolibrary **p36 (top)**; Peter Brooker/Rex Features **p36 (bottom)**; BILDHUSET AB/ Photolibrary **p37 (top)**; SRK/ Rex Features **p37 (bottom)**; Jochen Tack/ Alamy **p49**; Jon Buckle/ Empics Sports Photo Agency **p50 (top)**; Simon Stanmore, 2006/photographersdirect.com **p50 (bottom)**; Bob Battersby/ www.bdi-images.com **p56**; Index Stock Imagery/ Photolibrary **p58**; Last Resort Picture Library **p64**; Index Stock Imagery/ Photolibrary **p81**; Ken McKay/ Rex Features **p95**; Photononstop/ Photolibrary **p109**; Photononstop/ Photolibrary **p110**; Leslie Garland Picture Library/ Alamy **p150**; Workbook, Inc./ Photolibrary **p151**; Index Stock Imagery/ Photolibrary **p182**.

Introduction

'Using ICT' can be studied on its own or as a basis for further learning. DiDA is a suite of qualifications that allows you stop or carry on to a level that suits you. The qualification starts with 'Using ICT'; then you can move on to the next areas of study, which are:

- Multimedia
- Graphics
- Enterprise and businesses

Whatever you decide to do you must work on and pass the Using ICT qualification first.

What you need to learn in order to obtain the qualification is all covered in this book; the specific areas of learning are:

- Using information sources
- Using surveys
- Information handling
- Working with information
- Presenting information
- Paper publications
- On-screen publications
- Prototyping and testing
- Creating the portfolio
- Managing your project
- Review and evaluation
- Standard ways of working

Marking your work

You are assessed only on the portfolio.

The portfolio should be a storage system for your work. This is sent to a moderator to look through and assess. The portfolio is very important, as it is the only way the work can be assessed. Therefore it needs to be easy to find files or folders and should include everything that is necessary. There is no other way you will communicate your work to the moderator.

During the course you will learn new skills and enhance those you already have.

For the qualification you will need ICT skills in the following areas:

- Artwork and image-editing software
- Database software
- Digital sound
- Email
- Internet and intranets
- Presentation software
- Spreadsheet software
- Web-authoring software
- Word-processing software
- Summative project brief

The final piece of work for Unit 1, the SPB (summative project brief), will ask you to solve several problems, using your ICT skills learnt during the course. The brief, which will be sent to you, will tell you what you need to do. The questions in the brief should take around 30 hours to complete. You will need to produce evidence for the SPB and you will be awarded marks for this evidence. The work will go into your e-portfolio. The e-portfolio is a collection of your work stored digitally in a computer or computer system; none of your work will need to be saved on or printed out on paper.

The SPB is the only part of the DiDA course you will be assessed on externally, so it is very important that your work is planned and saved carefully. For your SPB you will be awarded marks which will be checked internally and externally.

How can computers damage our health or safety?

Computers are very safe machines if handled well and situated in the correct environment. If not, over a period of time, they can damage bones, muscles and eyes. Studies of thousands of computer users who worked in many different industries found that many workstations were poorly designed; this resulted in stress and fatigue among users.

Seating is one of the prime causes of discomfort and is linked to the back being in the 'C' position instead of the natural 'S' position. When you sit at a computer for long periods of time this will cause discomfort. It is vital that the chair/stool, desk, keyboard, and so on are positioned in such a way that the operator is comfortable for the maximum amount of time. Repetitive strain injury (RSI) is not a new illness, but it is known to have links with poorly positioned keyboards.

Tired or itchy eyes

This can occur if the eyes have been focused for a long time on an object that is nearby. In this situation we tend not to blink as often as we would normally, which results in the eyes failing to be refreshed. This has been linked to poor lighting and lack of breaks in viewing the VDU.

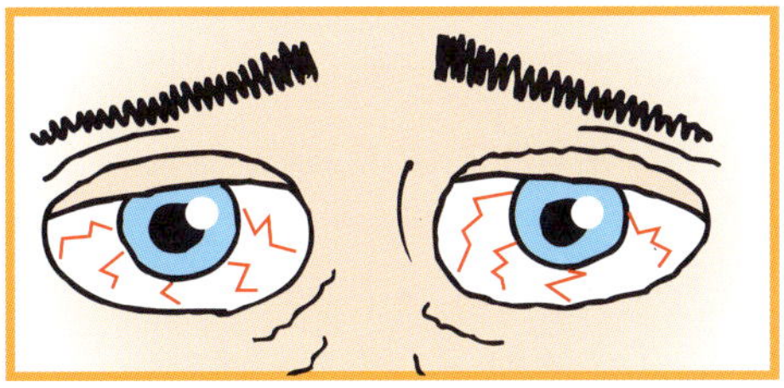

Screens on computers do give off *very small* amounts of radiation. The amount, however, falls well below the permissible amount allowed by international radiation safety groups. The soft x-rays actually travel only a few inches away from the monitor tubes before they dissipate so are unlikely to cause harmful side effects.

Lighting

The position of lighting and reduction of reflective light are both important considerations when positioning a computer. Because computer displays are self-lighting, users probably need less lighting rather than more. Positioning a computer in front of a window can cause glare on the screen, which causes rapid eye fatigue. Many offices now use uplighters, which bounce soft light off the ceiling rather than shine directly at people.

Printers

Laser printers give off ozone gas – a mild irritant – as a by-product of the electro-photographic process. This will not present a problem if the printer is set up in a well ventilated position.

The design of workstations

The best workstation is one which provides the user with the greatest comfort and safety. The key to this is to ensure the body is in a normal rather than abnormal position. If ergonomic data (information about average sizes and shapes of people) is used to design furniture and equipment, the eyes, neck, hands, wrists, arms and backs of legs are less likely to suffer any damage. Designers and office equipment manufacturers all use ergonomic data that is readily available. The charts give averages sizes, reach, height, and so on for men, women and children of all ages.

General health and safety

Your establishment or county will have very clear guidelines on health and safety issues in ICT suites. These are very general guidelines, but you must ensure that you follow them.

If you are not comfortable or you feel that your body is under strain while you are working, take a break. Tell your teacher, as they need to be aware of your discomfort.

Rules:

- Arrange the workstation so that your back is S-shaped, arms and hands horizontal, screen at arm's length.
- If your screen flickers, do not use it – a flickering screen can cause headaches and eye strain much more quickly than a flicker-free screen.

- Take regular breaks – do not sit in front of the machine for more than 20 minutes without moving.
- Get up and walk around or do some stretching exercises every 30 minutes.
- Have regular drinks of water – but bear in mind that water and electricity don't mix! Move away from your workstation to drink.

CHAPTER 1 Using information sources

What you will learn in this chapter

You will learn how to collect information from different sources, and how to record and store it.

It is very easy to spend too long on research. Sometimes we find it interesting to carry out research and get absorbed in finding more and more, without realising we have run out of time. This chapter will help you to find the things that you want, and only what you want. If you plan your time, which is always a good idea, you will focus on what you need and sift through information to get the bits you want. Do not simply assume you can go to the **Internet** and find everything – information is available from many other sources, like books, **CD**s, videos, **DVD**s, magazines and newspapers. The most common reason for running out of time is over-researching your subject. The maximum marks you can get for this area is 7 marks.

Information sources: what are they? They are anything or anybody who can help you to research and be informed about the subject you wish to work on. Without the right information you cannot hope to get your projects or work to look, sound or read well.

The days when you could get marks for collecting photos and text from catalogues or using Internet printouts to prove that you have done your research are long gone. Today you must show that you have used a range of sources to obtain information that is relevant (useful to you) and very focused towards your work.

Collecting information for your projects shows your teacher and the moderator that you know what you are doing because you have researched your brief and you are informed. Information also helps you to understand what you need to do and it usually makes life a lot easier. A well-researched project is usually the result of careful use of information.

Storing information

With the DiDA qualification nothing needs to be written on paper. So usually you would save what you have been working on in an electronic format. However, this does not mean you can never get your research information from papers, magazines, book, sketches or diagrams that you have drawn. These can still be stored on computer by **scanning** or photographing them.

Before you even start collecting data you should learn how to store it on your computer. To make materials suitable for electronic storage you can:

- Scan
- Photograph
- Place information on a CD, DVD or **floppy disk**
- Drag or copy images into a word-processed document

You can store on a computer:

- Sounds
- Images (pictures)
- Photos
- Movies
- Text

1 Using information sources

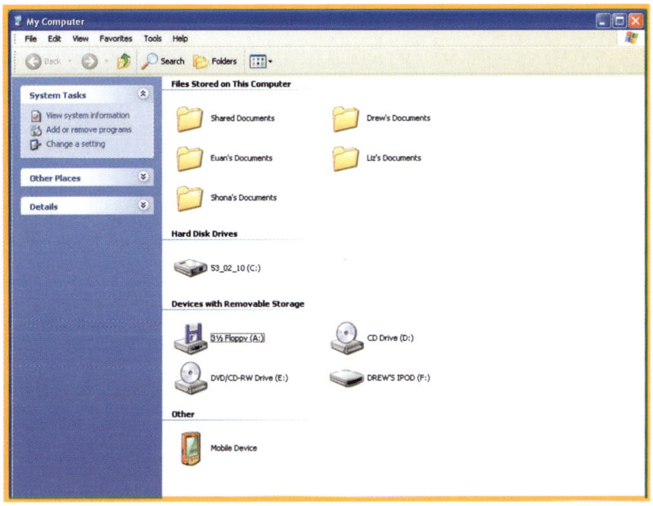

You can store information in different ways on the computer:

- On floppy disks
- On rewriteable CDs
- On the **hard disk**
- In **user area**s of a **network**
- In attached **file**s sent by **email**

Right-click the mouse click on the desktop to make a folder

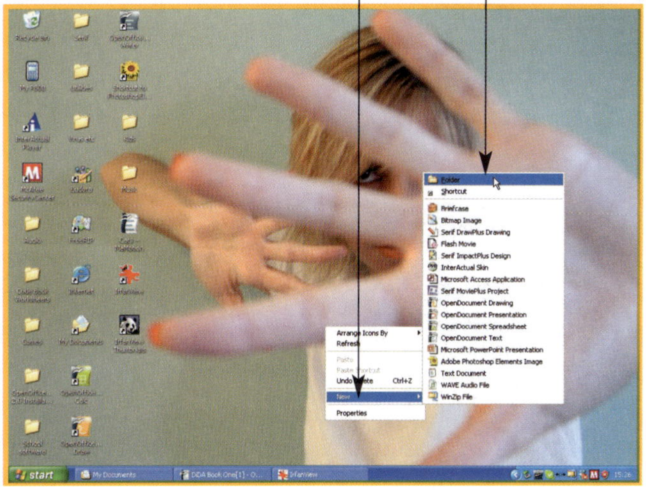

Folders

Storing files in **folder**s means you can create an organised saving and **retrieval** system. Perhaps you might have one for text, one for images, one for a specific project, and so on. Files can be saved or dragged into folders.

In a program such as Micorsoft Word® you can make new folders when saving.

Sounds

Sound can be recorded using Microsoft® Sound Recorder **software**, found in the *Windows*® **operating system** on a **PC**, if you have a microphone.

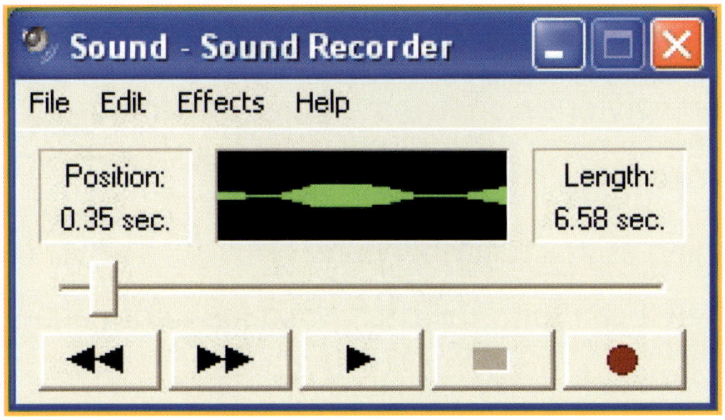

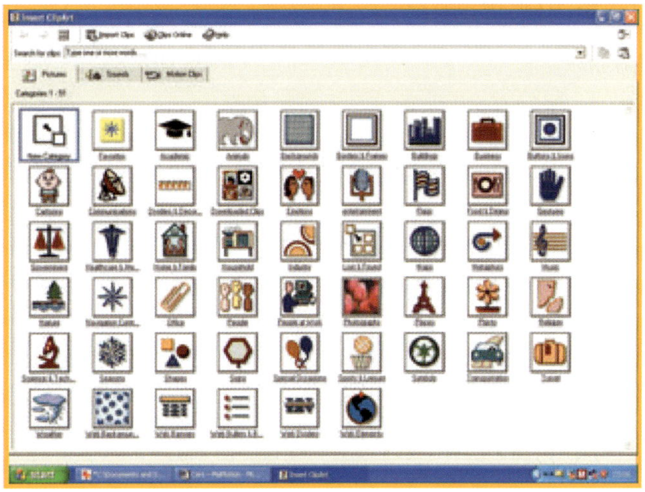

Images can be scanned in to most Microsoft® programs; try it in the Microsoft *Word*® word- processing program by going to Insert picture, from scanner or cameras. Most Microsoft software has a large range of clip art (pictures already drawn or photographed and stored for your use).

All these methods can be used to illustrate or help explain your work.

Why do you need information?

You need information in DiDA because you cannot make any sound decisions until you are informed. The people who assess your work will know if your work has been researched, and in any case it usually makes life easier if you understand what you are working on or towards. In industry, any large company would get as much information as possible about the people their new products are designed for, find out about costs, legal issues, environmental considerations, what conditions the new products would be used in, and so on.

They would ***always*** do market research and never make any decisions on the colour, shape, lettering, cost, size, layout, taste, smell, texture, and so on, until they knew the market their product was aimed at. A product could be anything from socks to a sports car, or a tube of toothpaste.

Plus:

- Your work becomes more relevant.
- The information you receive may help you make the right decisions.
- It is easier if you know what you are talking about.
- You get to know your market.

How or where can you get information?

Information is gathered through either primary or secondary methods. **Secondary** information is that which already exists, for instance the Internet, telephone, books, specialist magazines, libraries, and so on. **Primary** information may be obtained from:

- **Observation** – by watching something as it actually happens
- **Questionnaire** – if this is well written it can form the basis of sound information capture

- **Work-study** – going and watching experts at work
- **Interview** – many experts are happy to talk about their subjects.

Interviews

People you know who have specialist knowledge may be able to help through being interviewed. This may be recorded in many ways. While the person is talking you could record the interview on video, sound recorder or by notes, either done on a **laptop** or by paper and pen. Any of these methods can be saved into the computer. You could make a special folder for interview notes.

Plan your interview carefully: the people you interview may be very busy and would always appreciate a well-planned interview, rather than a list of random or irrelevant questions.

- Ask specific questions that will help you become informed.
- Plan time for photos or movies.
- Interviews can be done over the phone or through Microsoft Messenger® for instant responses. You could also use email or carry out the research in person.

In almost all situations, a combination of methods could be used in order to get the best quality information possible. In industry you can even *buy* information! There are specialist firms who have information on people's buying habits. They can tell you which areas of the country have more of this and less of that, which areas spend more on what, and so on.

Other sources of information you may find helpful

- Media (TV, videos, CDs, radio, DVDs)
- Trade events, exhibitions and fairs, conventions
- Government statistics
- Demographics – details of people's habits and economic activity

Gathering information can take time and space so you need to go through it thoroughly and reject anything that is unlikely to be relevant to your work. Large amounts do not mean large marks!

Information checks

Check your information is up to date and check the sources. For example, your friends may give you information about hobbies, sports or other interests, which may or may not be reliable or accurate. The information you get from radio or TV and newspapers may be biased. That means they may slant the information in a way that suits their purpose rather than being totally truthful. Do not believe everything you read!

Making notes

Whether you are working from the Internet or from a library book, selecting information and writing it down in note form, either on a word processor or with pen and paper, often reinforces the new knowledge the information is yielding. If you work on paper, your notes can be scanned into your computer and saved, or typed in at a later date.

Books usually have an index which is set out alphabetically (a to z) and you can quickly look through this to find the letter associated with the information you are trying to obtain. Indexes are there to save you time.

TV can sometimes be a great source of information – especially as so many of us have a huge number of TV channels to choose from. There are often programmes that contain very helpful information. This can be recorded and clips can be transferred to your PC. This is easy if you can record onto DVD, as many computers now accept these.

Educational institutions such as schools or colleges often have an **audio-visual** department that may be able to help you with recording, providing you give them advance warning. So look though the TV guides every now and then.

Using the Internet

This is a brilliant way to get information about anything, but how can you decide what information you need from the thousands of pages offered by **search engines** such as Google™? First, be specific: type in exactly what you want. Sometimes the first pages suggested are irrelevant, so look through them but do not spend too long on them – learn to be decisive and work quickly. You could literally spend years looking at information. If you find a good source you can highlight what you need, then **copy and paste** it into a word-processed document. Providing the copied work is for your own educational use **copyright** problems should not be an issue, but do bear in mind that anything you use must be acknowledged.

If you find a brilliant **website** that you may need to return to, record its address.

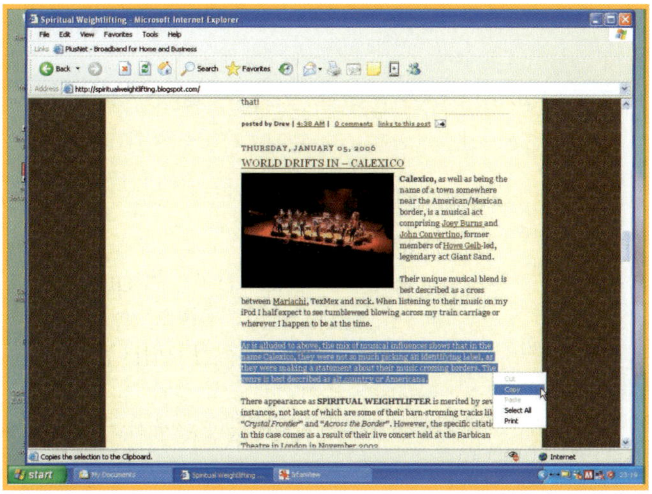

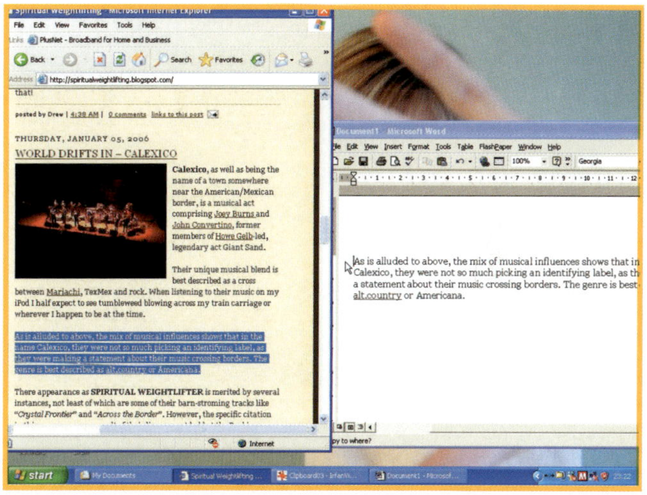

Saving favourites

If you find a good site and wish to store it, you can **drag** the web address into the Favorites or Bookmarks section. Next time you need that site you can simply go to Favorites or Bookmarks and double-click on the site name. This will automatically link you to that site.

In Microsoft *Word* ® you can make a list of relevant or useful sites by simply typing out the full web address; this will turn blue. If you click on this blue text, providing you have access to the Internet, you will be taken directly to that site. For example:

www.bbc.co.uk
www.learn2.co.uk
www.hodderheadline.co.uk

Before using the Internet read this!

Using information sources on the Internet

There is lots of material available on the Internet. Unlike traditional media (e.g. books, magazines, television), no one has to check the content before it is made public. It is your job as a researcher to decide if the material you find is from a trusted source, is telling the whole truth and is reliable.

Searching for information

When looking for information (researching), you should ask yourself the following questions:

- Do I want purely factual information?
- Do I want people's opinions?

- Do I want the points of view of others that may help me to make a decision?
- Do I want eyewitness reports?
- Do I need information to support my ideas or to get ideas about what others think?

There are so many web pages now, from just about every country in the world. This information is all accessible from your computer – you could say there is too much information! So how do you get what you need? How can you reject what you do not need and save yourself time and effort?

Using the web for research

The easiest way to search out your information and to get to it fast is to use a search engine. Search engines are the tools we use to find sources of information on the web. Search engines include Yahoo and Google. The search engine does exactly what its name suggests: it searches the web for words that you have entered. The words you enter tell the search engine what to look for. If you load up Google (www.google.co.uk), and enter text, the more information you enter, the more you are likely to find exactly what you are looking for.

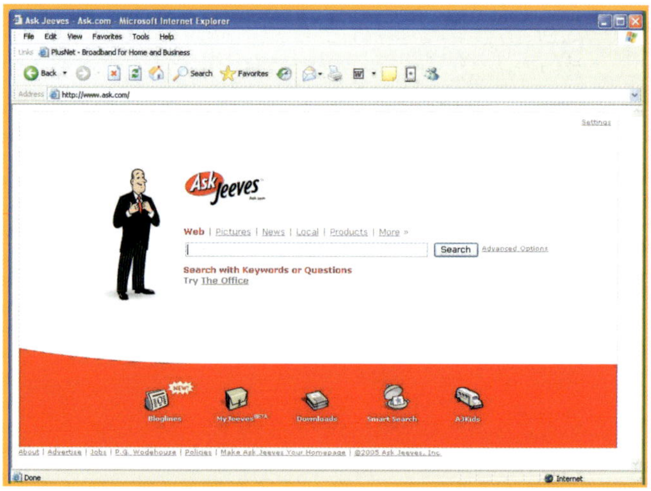

For example, if you are looking for a seller of Dutch, white, long-eared mice, based in Essex, enter all those words. If you just type in 'white mice' you are unlikely to find Dutch long-eared mice living in Essex, the reason being you are not being specific enough. So be **specific**. Search engines are sophisticated and are much easier to use than they used to be. They are also much faster than they were previously, so providing you put as much detail as possible into the search box it will probably find what you are looking for.

Images

If you are looking for images or photos, select the 'Images' option that Google offers and you will search for images but not text. All search engines have help options, which are really worth reading before you start to use them. Not all search engines work in the same way. Google will help you if you misspell a word, and suggest what it thinks you are attempting to spell. For instance, if you spell rabbit 'rabit', it will probably work out what you are looking for and suggest the correct spelling.

Before you start to search for information on the web it is worth getting a piece of paper and making a quick list of what you are looking for, checking you know the correct spelling, deciding whether or not you need text, images or both, finding a system for storing the information and rejecting what you do not need.

If you have trouble finding something you need information on, check the following:

- Try re-evaluating the name or words
- Try narrowing or broadening the search
- Try a different search engine.

How to find information on the Internet

1. *Define the information you need and state it as a question*: Start by writing your information need in words. Make a list on paper if you think this will help. This will help you to think about what you need and to think of suitable search terms. If you need help defining a word then look in a dictionary.
2. *Identify and prioritise keywords*: You need to identify suitable terms to represent the words from part 1. You should choose words that describe the topic, and you should also list words and ideas you do *not* want included. These are called 'keywords'. You can list keywords and alternative terms in a table:

FORD
CAR
EDSEL

Evaluating the search process

Always check the results you are getting and the information sent; never just use it without thinking – you must make absolutely sure it is relevant information. Remember to store useful sites by **bookmarking** them as they can be used again simply by going to Favorites.

The more information you get the more you may think you need to search, but this is not always the case! If the Internet is just not working for you it is not the end of the world – try another method. The library is a great source of information, particularly when it comes to local issues.

Now you have found what you are looking for!

If you have found what you are looking for on the Internet and have stored or read the information, you need to decide what is of use to you. You also need to decide if the information is honest and truthful – is the content accurate? Is it set at the right level for your work? How long ago was this information placed on the web? If it is old the information may be out of date and no longer correct. Constantly changing items, such as design, music fashion, vehicles or travel, require information to be as up to date as possible.

It is vital to evaluate the search process at all stages. Sometimes you cannot find relevant information because of a poorly constructed search strategy, wrong search terms, poor retrieval methods or the wrong source.

This can also apply to times when too much material is retrieved. Too few, too many or inappropriate search results could mean:

- You need to rethink the search terms.
- You need to narrow/broaden the scope of your search(es).
- You need to try different types of sources.

Copyright

When someone takes a photo or writes in a book, magazine or newspaper they are the owners of its copyright. This means that if anyone else wanted to use parts or all of the work they would have to ask for permission to do so. If they did not they could be infringing the creator's copyright, which is illegal.

A good example is Disney. Walt Disney invented and drew Mickey Mouse, so the copyright belonged to him, and now belongs to his company. Disney may let people use their characters (such as Mickey Mouse), but ask for payment each time it is used. So a company printing sweatshirts with Mickey Mouse on must ask Disney first if they can use the image and pay money for every shirt Mickey is printed on. Sometimes people use famous logos to produce fakes or copies of well-known brands without permission. By doing so they risk having their goods confiscated and having to pay heavy fines. While you are working on your projects you may want to use text, images or logos from a variety of sources. Sometimes they might be copyright-free and in the **public domain**. Sometimes, if they are to be used for educational purposes, fees are not required. However, **this is not always the case**, so you should always check the copyright terms carefully for any material that you wish to reproduce. If in any doubt, **check with your tutor**.

How to get good marks

How difficult is it to get good marks? Well, it is not really difficult if you use common sense and work logically.

- ✓ Find your own information and make it clear that you have done so.
- ✓ Make sure information is useful and not just filling up space.
- ✓ You should, if possible, create some multimedia sections.
- ✓ Check surveys and other data carefully.
- ✓ Do not copy someone else's work: you will be found out!
- ✓ Try to think of good ways to get your information by yourself, if possible.
- ✓ Information is all around us; find and use the right sources.
- ✓ Use both self-selected secondary sources and those suggested in the summative project brief.
- ✓ Remember where you got your information from and make sure you can use it without infringing **copyright** law.
- ✓ Large chunks of irrelevant data are useless.
- ✓ Make sure you save regularly and not just at the end of each lesson. **Save your work as soon as you start and name it**. Remember where you saved it (on a disk, in your user area, on a CD-ROM or on the hard drive).

Homework

1 Ask a search engine to find something silly, like spearmint doughnuts or inflatable shoes. See what information comes up. Is it relevant? Is it useful? Break the information down into a 30-word report.

2 Ask a friend to suggest a search, trying to limit the number of hits to under 1000.

3 Decide on a favourite film or record that you think is really brilliant. Ask 10 people you know, some of different ages, what they think of it. List your findings and see if a trend develops.

	Liked	Disliked	OK	Rubbish	Never heard of it
Age 17	✓				
15		✓			

Create a simple graph in Excel to show the results graphically.

4 Using the results from question 3, create a simple pie chart of your findings using Microsoft *Word®*. See Chapter 19 for help with Microsoft *Word®*.

CHAPTER 2

Using surveys

What you will learn in this chapter

You will learn how to carry out market research and to design a questionnaire to find out people's likes, dislikes, purchasing patterns and lifestyles.

'Knowledge is power'. This statement was made by Francis Bacon around 400 years ago, and modern technology has proved him right. Most of the energy expended by ICT specialists is to gather data and then analyse or use it in a certain way, so as to develop knowledge. Data is often obtained from conducting surveys.

Chapter 1 was concerned with how to use information; this chapter will take you through developing methods of collecting useful data, which can in turn be used as information.

Business can be divided into various sectors:

- Agriculture
- Construction
- Chemicals
- Food and drink
- Fuel and power
- Metals

- Minerals
- Nuclear industry
- Pulp and paper
- Radioactive substance users
- Textiles and tanneries
- Waste management
- Water
- Wood

Each of these includes a wide range of companies, organisations and agencies (to investigate these sectors further, visit http://www.environment-agency.gov.uk/business/).

Businesses often gather useful data through surveys and then use that data to help inform decisions. To do this a company will often employ a specialist or hire an external agency to carry out market research.

Market research

Market research is an important exercise in developing a product or service. A typical market research investigation might look into the possibility of launching a new product line in a supermarket.

Hodder Cakes Survey – **Research Sheet**

Questions that the results of the survey should help me answer:

1. How many people visit the bakery department each week?

   ____

2. What kind of cakes do they buy?

   ____

3. What flavour cakes do they buy?

   ____

4. Do they buy cakes for themselves or for other people?

   ____

A supermarket manager has been approached by the head of the bakery department, after a few customers have asked for a new variety of cake. The manager passes this request for a new line to his area manager, who instigates a research project.

The research project is to be handled by an external agency, so a meeting is called between the market research agency and a number of the supermarket staff. This meeting sets the boundaries for possible surveys:

- What products can be suggested?
- What is the potential customer group?
- Are there any regional differences to be considered?
- Where will the research take place?
- How long will it take to get a result from the market research?
- What is the budget?

There are many other questions that will be discussed at such a meeting.

When the ground rules have been set, the market research agency will start to develop their strategy. In this instance they will be carrying out a survey of a range of customers as they leave the supermarkets. The first thing they must do is decide on the sort of data they need to gather, so that they will obtain information that can be passed to the supermarket.

This 'theme' is relatively broad: what sort of cake would be a good product to sell from the bakery counter in a supermarket? The skill of the researcher is to be able to break this down into more useful sections.

Questioning

The simplest level of data is in a **binary** form – yes or no, one or nought. If all questions asked can be broken down to a binary or 'closed' answer, then the data will be simple to collate and analyse statistically. Therefore the researchers will try to break down the information required into a sequence of yes/no questions and answers.

For example:

Have you ever bought a cake from the bakery department? Yes/No

Another aspect of survey design is linking questions together to develop a pattern in the answers. If the answer to one question is yes, the following question probes further; if it is no, the respondent moves to a different question:

1. Have you ever bought a cake from the bakery department? Yes/No
If you have answered Yes, go to question 2; if you have answered No, go to question 7.
2. Have you bought a cake from the bakery department in the last week? Yes/No
3. …
4. …
5. …
6. …
7. Do you buy any of the following items?
Ice cream
Custard
etc.

When you have developed the basic structure, taking into account the two factors above – closed questions and relationships between questions – it is time to start designing the complete questionnaire. Raw data, such as whether or not someone has bought a cake, is the main part of the survey, but to give a clearer picture you need to collect more general data, such as the gender, age and occupation of the respondent.

These closed questions are straightforward, both to ask and to record the responses. But sometimes more complex data may need to be collected. In the case of the new cake, a particular taste or texture may be an important aspect of the product design. This would be difficult to elicit through closed questions:

Do you like vanilla? Yes/No
Do you like strawberry? Yes/No
Do you like blackcurrant? Yes/No
Do you like cherry? Yes/No
etc.

It would be a lot easier and quicker to give a range of answers and allow the respondent to choose one:

From this range, which flavour would be your favourite choice:
Vanilla, Strawberry, Blackcurrant, Cherry, …

Both of these would be preferable to:

What is your favourite flavour?

which could generate as many different responses as there are people to ask!

Another strategy for gathering complex data in a manageable form is to ask people to 'rank' something:

On a scale of 1 to 5 (1 being least favourite and 5 being most favourite) please score the following flavours:

Vanilla	**1 2 3 4 5**
Strawberry	**1 2 3 4 5**
Blackcurrant	**1 2 3 4 5**
Cherry	**1 2 3 4 5**
etc.	

At all times the researchers will try to avoid 'open' questions, such as:

Why do you buy cake?

The responses to that type of question often prove meaningless, as the respondents can give too many different answers. To be able to analyse the results later, the questions need to elicit useful and precise responses. Therefore, open questions must be avoided.

It is also important that the questions do not prompt a particular answer:

The most popular cake is the iced sponge – do you like it? Yes/No

This question may seem okay – it requires a closed response; but leading the question with a statement such as this will cause many people to state yes, as they are influenced by the popularity expressed in the statement. Most people like to feel that they fit in and so will tend to agree with popular answers.

Another aspect of 'leading' the response could be through omission – not offering a potential answer:

From the list below, please state which is your favourite colour:
Green
Blue
Yellow

By limiting the potential answers a false result could be obtained. Many people would normally state red as being their favourite colour, but the question does not allow that as a response. It also limits the respondent to choosing from the three options; therefore it does not actually ask for their *favourite* colour.

The questionnaire will be tested at various stages of development, to ensure that the questions are eliciting the expected responses. It is important that the data collected can generate the right information. Questions such as, 'Do you like cake?' may seem to be important, but if the respondent is the person who buys the cake, is it really important that *they* like cake? If they buy cake it may mean that someone in their household likes cake, but not necessarily them. This *could* mean that the results show that everyone who buys cake does not like it!

This may not be spotted in testing the questionnaire and may only show up when the results are analysed. This odd result is termed an **anomaly**. However, through careful testing and the experience of the market researchers most of the anomalies will be removed before the survey is carried out. Sometimes an anomaly can prove useful as it can open up a whole new area of research. If the question 'Do you like cake? is asked and the respondent states no, it may be that they do not like the cake that is available. A more accurate question would be, 'Do you like *Battenberg* cake?' Through thorough testing the questionnaire will be finalised and made ready for use.

In this instance the survey will be carried out by the market researchers, so the layout and appearance is perhaps not so important. However, a great deal of market research is carried out through postal questionnaires or leaflets that are filled in by the respondents. If this is the case, the layout and appearance is an essential element of the design.

Who is to be asked?

Where the survey is to be carried out has been decided at the outset – customers leaving the supermarket will be asked to take part. This is sometimes called an 'exit survey', as the respondents are *exiting* the place that the survey relates to.

The number of respondents also needs to be considered – the market researchers will have an idea of the number of responses they need to ensure a representative set of results. Very few surveys will seek more than a few hundred responses. Some surveys that are taken very seriously may only have data from a small sample group, perhaps 20 or 30 people. One of the national newspapers recently ran a survey to discuss whether the A level qualification should be kept in the future – there are around 500,000 students doing A levels, but only 1000 members of the public, over 18, were approached. Yet that was seen as a representative sample of a population of over 50 million. To launch a new product or check that an existing product or service is still fulfilling its need, a sample of 50 appropriate people will probably give enough useful data to proceed to the next stage, which may involve testing the product with a representative sample.

In the case of the new cake, if the item were expected to be sold in supermarkets all over the country it would be sensible to carry out research in different locations, as tastes around the country differ. If it were to be sold in only one store, it would not need the expensive outlay of surveying on a national scale. Products such as food items are often launched in one area of the country first. This enables the suppliers and retailers to check that the item is appropriate to their customer base. Although most supermarkets may look similar, they each cater for a different group of customers and so any new product needs to be right for that particular group, otherwise its sales will not be as high as they might be in another store.

When the survey has been carried out the results are carefully collated by the market research agency. These results will allow the researchers to group the data and put together a much more detailed set of responses. This information can then be passed back to the supermarket team, as a set of recommendations.

Use of IT

In recent years IT has become an essential element of collating and investigating results. It is now common practice for the results from a survey to be entered into a **spreadsheet**, where the raw data can be manipulated to provide graphs, charts and other illustrative materials for presenting the results. To find out more about spreadsheets see Chapter 17.

This is why the design of the questionnaire is so important. Simple yes or no answers can easily be recorded on a spreadsheet. As mentioned earlier, if more complex responses are required, it is often useful to provide a range of predesignated answers, as in multiple- choice questions, or numerical 'scores', as in ranking questions. This means that a letter or number signifying the response can be recorded in the spreadsheet.

Certain types of data can be represented in different ways, which can influence the reader.

The following table contains data from a survey. The graphs in Figure 2.6 illustrate the same thing, but they look very different and appear to tell a different story!

Question	A	B	C	D	E	No answer
1	3	3	4	2	3	5
2	3	4	2	2	2	7
3	6	3	1	2	2	6
4	2	4	2	4	1	7
5	2	2	3	3	4	6

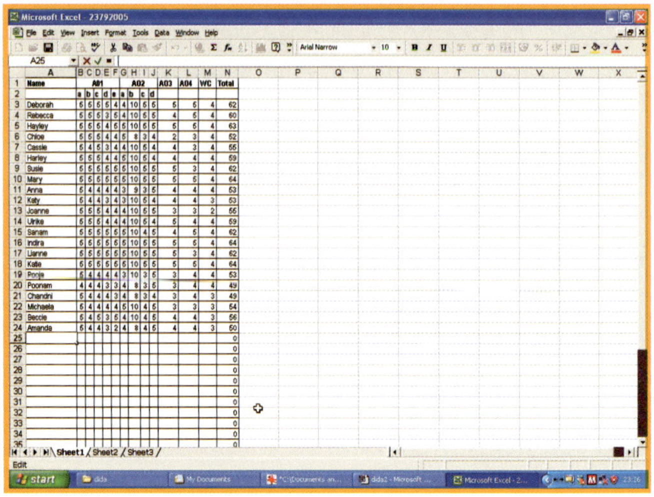

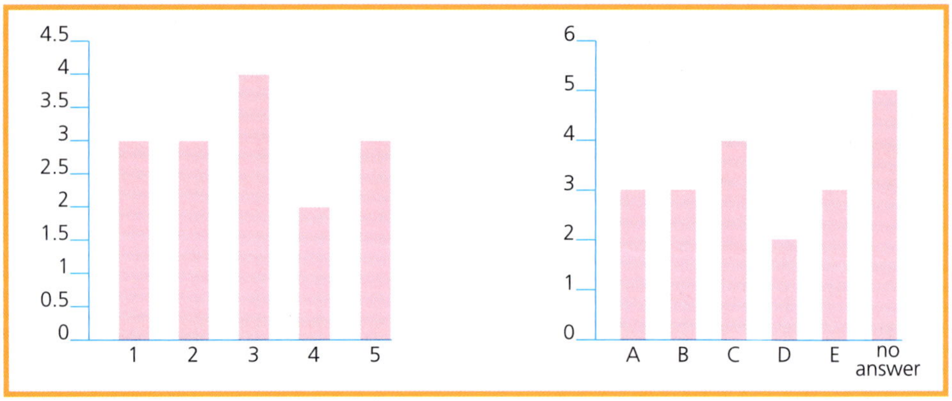

Figure 2.6 Graphs of the answers to the survey

The inclusion of the final column of data skews the results – the largest single group of respondents did not offer an answer. But the lack of answer is an important response, as it can tell the researcher a great deal.

There is also an element of showmanship in presenting data. Remember that data on its own is not a lot of use; it is when it has been manipulated that it becomes information – and the manipulation is the bit that can make the information tell a particular story.

Presenting the results

In the case of the new cake the data will probably be presented in a paper-based document. However, there are various methods that can be employed for different purposes and audiences.

In presenting data the general rule is to keep it simple. If a table of data has been collected, present it as a table. If the data is to be presented in a document, it is important that the table fits on one page, or that any page breaks are positioned carefully so that it is still easy to read the data.

3.06
3.40
3.45
3.46
2.52
4.00

It is important that the data can be read easily from the table – careful choice of **font** and layout is essential, and text must be left-aligned. If numerical data is displayed there are rules on the positioning of the numbers within the **cells** – they must be right-aligned, and if decimal places are to be shown, the decimal points should be aligned vertically. If these rules are not followed it can make the data very difficult to read.

Although it is sometimes the only way to add labels, if text is to be vertically aligned it should be rotated, rather than placed one letter above the other.

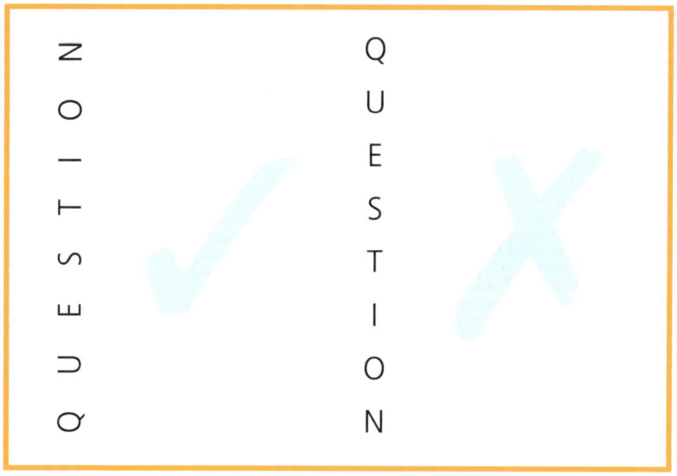

Most spreadsheet applications offer a variety of preset formats for the layout of the table, including careful use of colour. If there are totals in a particular column, it is good practice to have that column on the extreme right. All 'total' rows should be located at the bottom of tables, to avoid confusion.

The greatest advantage of using a spreadsheet application is that the data can be manipulated quickly and easily. Although a word processor can generate a table, and make the results look clear, it is the numerical functionality that makes a spreadsheet so useful. The simplest functions are to total up columns or rows, but most spreadsheet applications can carry out much more complex mathematical functions. Microsoft *Excel*®, for example, has over 200 functions or formulas built in to it, and each of those can be altered by the user to achieve a particular outcome.

Usually it would be the market research agency that would manipulate the data to achieve a set of results that could be presented to the supermarket team. This is because the supermarket team would probably not be skilled in working with raw data. (Raw data is information that has not been sorted or ordered in any way.)

When the data has been compiled and manipulated, it would be presented as a report to the supermarket team. This report would also include a number of recommendations that have been arrived at by the researchers. As the researchers

would not necessarily have detailed knowledge of the development of products at the supermarket, the suggestion would be purely to do with the data that had been collected from the survey.

Therefore, in the case of the new cake, if the majority of respondents said they would like a new product the recommendation would reflect this, whereas the supermarket staff may need more than a statistical majority to go ahead and develop a new product, as this can be a costly exercise. They would want to include information from their own experiences, such as the success or failure of previous new product launches, sales figures and other data.

These recommendations, along with sales figures and other data held by the supermarket team, will be turned into a final proposal. This may then lead to the development of a new product or, as is more often the case, the recommendations could lead to cancelling the proposed change.

How to get good marks

- ✓ **Make sure your survey is relevant to your project.**
- ✓ **Survey forms should be clear and easy to follow, otherwise people will not fill them in, so design them well.**
- ✓ **Plan out your strategy for market research. Surveys can tell you some things, but make sure you use other methods of information gathering too.**
- ✓ **Make sense of the information you have gained and show it was a useful exercise.**

Homework

1 Find examples of 'open' and 'closed' questions – if you study the way your teachers ask questions, they will often start by asking open questions, such as, 'Who can tell me how the scanner works?', but students do not like answering open questions so the teacher usually moves to asking closed questions, such as, 'Does this printer use ink or toner?'

2 Make a detailed list of the stages that the development of a survey or questionnaire would normally go through.

3 Plan a survey of your own, such as an investigation into the hobbies and pastimes of your colleagues. Develop a questionnaire that can be distributed to the respondents and then collate the data from the responses. Present the information in three different ways, to be suitable for reading by three different and distinct audiences: your colleagues, the local council department responsible for supporting youth activities and parents.

4 Carry out an Internet search for products that have failed. You could look up the Ford Edsel car, which was manufactured at enormous cost but then failed to sell. Write a short report explaining why this product was not successful.

5 Another massive failure was the Sinclair C5 car which was designed and produced in the early 1980s. What went wrong? Write a short report.

6 What kind or survey sheet do you think would have been used to see if people thought the Sinclair C5 was a good idea?

Give reasons for your answer.

7 Spend a little time looking at this site, which covers market research for businesses: http://www.researchindex.co.uk/market-research. There is a lot of useful information and guidelines on this site, some set up by the government to help businesses succeed.

CHAPTER 3

Information handling

What you will learn in this chapter

You will learn how to develop and use a simple database.

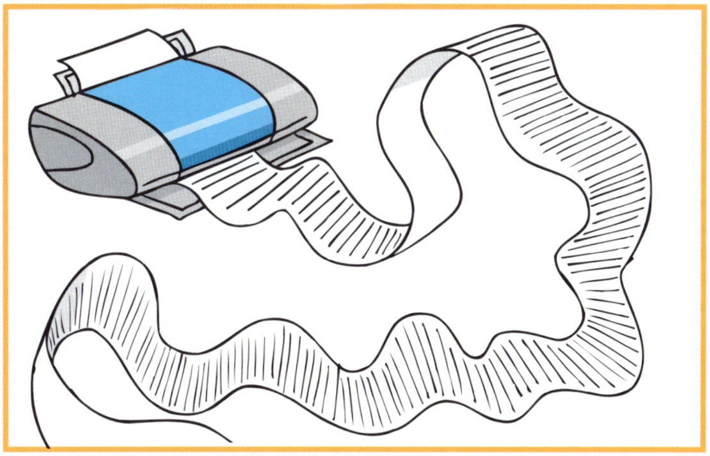

The previous chapter related to carrying out surveys and recording the data in spreadsheet form. This is fine for relatively small amounts of data that do not necessarily have any links to other data sets. If greater amounts of data are to be stored and manipulated, then you need to use a different, and in some ways more complex, piece of software – a **database**.

The supermarket mentioned in the last chapter would normally hold vast amounts of information about products, suppliers, customers and other things. This information can be captured when customers pay at the till. Although a spreadsheet can be used as a database, and the collection of results from the survey mentioned in the last chapter is a form of database, it would be a limited method of storing and accessing the sort of information normally held by the supermarket.

Businesses rely heavily on data. It is essential in modern commerce.

Suppliers need to ensure that they keep precise records of all transactions, so that they can charge the correct amount to the correct customer, and also deliver the correct items to the correct customer. In the nineteenth century the Industrial

> 'It is a capital mistake to theorise before one has data.' Sir Arthur Conan Doyle (author of Sherlock Holmes mysteries)

Revolution took place. This caused people to move from rural occupations and homes into towns and cities, where they gained employment in factories. One of the side effects of this change was that suppliers were no longer local to their customers. Goods and services could be transported further and more quickly than previously. This meant that more detailed records needed to be kept by the suppliers. Various systems were developed, usually based around cards containing regular sets of data, for example:

Customer Name
Address
Purchase
Cost
Billed
Paid

Until recently, this system was still used in many organisations. However, over the last 20 years information technology (IT) has taken over in most companies.

The data stored on these cards was easily located and read. It was also relatively straightforward to update, amend or delete. Unfortunately, as the customer base increased, the size of the database increased to a point where it became less easy to use. This difficulty led to the invention that was a cornerstone of the development of computers – the punched card system. Weaving looms had used cards with holes punched in them in particular places for some time. These cards told the machine what pattern to weave into the materials it was making.

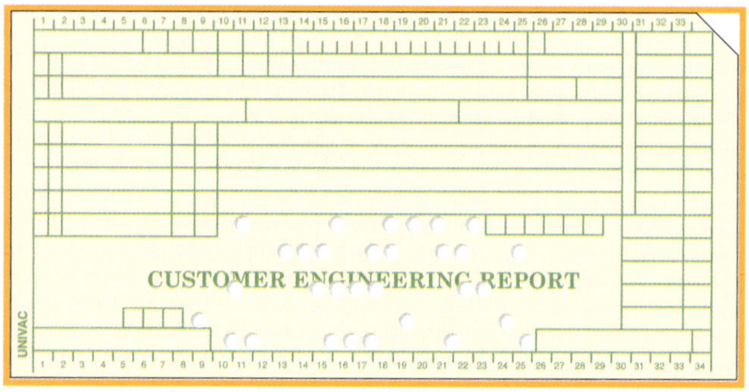

The system was altered slightly and used to record the 1890 American Census, by Dr Herman Hollerith. The card system he developed consisted of a card with holes punched in specific places that recorded the name, address, age and relationships of every man, woman and child in the USA, approximately 62 million people. These cards could be read by an electronic device which then recorded the data. This was the first major database to be manipulated electronically.

From this point the use of electronics to store and manipulate data has moved on to what we have today. But the basic principle remains: that certain bits of fixed data can be recorded, but it must be done in a uniform or consistent way.

Database structure

Every database is constructed from a set of records; each record is made up from a number of fields.

Before developing a database the nature of the data to be stored must be investigated. A simple address book database is a good place to start. Normally an address book contains the following information:

Name
Address

But the advantage of using a database to store the information is that it can be searched and manipulated easily, so the address book needs to be much more complex, to make it easier later!

Before deciding on the format of the database it is important to work out what you want to be able to get from it. Although its primary task is to store information, it is not much good if the information cannot be found and retrieved easily. Collecting data from the survey described in Chapter 2 is one thing, locking it away in a cupboard and throwing away the key would be a bit pointless – but that can happen if the data is not stored in a useful manner.

If you add in more fields at this point, the information you can access later will be much easier to find:

First name
Initial
Second name
House number
Street name
Town
County

Postcode
Phone number
Mobile number
Email address
Notes

If you do not separate the first name and second name fields, it would be impossible to find someone with a particular second name, '**Dave**' and '**Parry**' would be two separate searchable entries in this database. Without separation my name would still be '**Dave Parry**', but the computer would not be able to find the Parry part!

Good	
First Name	Dave
Second Name	Parry

Bad	
Name	Dave Parry

The same rule covers all fields. When you have come up with what you think are the field names you want to use, take another look – can you break them down further? If you do this now it will make the database much more useful later. It is a lot easier to add fields now than it will be when the database is populated and you realise that you should have had a separate field for house number!

Now that you have a more detailed set of fields to hold the data for each record, you need to think about what to do with it. On card records the data had to be laid out in a way that would make it easy to find a particular entry quickly – such as putting the surname at the top so that it was visible when a user flicked through the cards. An electronic database will need similar indexing.

In the case of an address book the second name is usually the single most important detail, but because of the way database applications work, it probably does not matter to the software. In fact, it can be confusing, as there may be more than one entry with the same second name. However, it is good practice to add an indexing number or 'primary key' to the record so that the software can easily locate a particular record.

Next you need to think about what type of data will be recorded in each field.

First name	**text, probably up to 12 letters**
Initial	**text 1 letter**
Second name	**text up to 10 letters**

House number	number up to 3 digits
Street name	text up to 20 letters
Town	text up to 20 letters
County	text up to 20 letters
Postcode	text and numbers in a particular sequence
Phone number	number up to 11 digits
Mobile number	number up to 11 digits
Email address	text up to 30 letters
Notes	text up to 150 letters

At this point the basic structure of a record is set: each record contains 12 preset fields that require data to be entered. The record will also contain a 'primary key' field that the computer will assign automatically.

This design will allow for the recording of names and addresses. Because of the functions of a database it should be possible to search the database for the record of an individual, by any of the fields. For example, if the database has been completed it would be possible to search for any record that contained the number '9' in the house number field. The software would then return every record with the matching '9'.

Data entry

Data entry is the most problematic part of building a database. It is easy to make a mistake and, without careful checking, that mistake can go unnoticed. This can create terrible problems later.

If a simple error such as misspelling a name goes unnoticed it could mean that the record containing that name does not get included in any results from searches. That means that if the address book database is searched for anybody with the name Parry, and if the data entry had spelt it 'Prray' by mistake, the record would not be found.

It is therefore essential that as many errors as possible are designed out of the database. This can be done by using 'validation rules'. These rules do not stop mistakes, but they make it more difficult for some mistakes to be made.

In the address book above, the house number is expected to be a number of up to three digits. The database application can be made to check the data as it is entered, to make sure that no text is entered and no more than three digits are entered. The fields for postcode, telephone and mobile numbers can also have rules applied to ensure that the correct structure of data is entered.

Other fields can be completed automatically, which ensures that mistakes are not made by entering the data manually. The county field can have a 'pick list' of counties. The 'initial' can be generated automatically from the first letter of the 'first name' field.

However, even with these validation rules and checks in place, the software cannot detect all possible errors. For example, the database cannot tell the difference between 'Dave' and 'David' or 'Dadiv'. It is therefore important that data is entered carefully and checked as it is entered.

In some cases it may be possible to import data sets from another application; the results from the survey in the previous chapter for instance. Most modern software has built-in converters so that common file formats can be **import**ed or **export**ed from one package to another. Most databases can understand spreadsheet data, but be careful when importing that the field names match, and the data format is compatible.

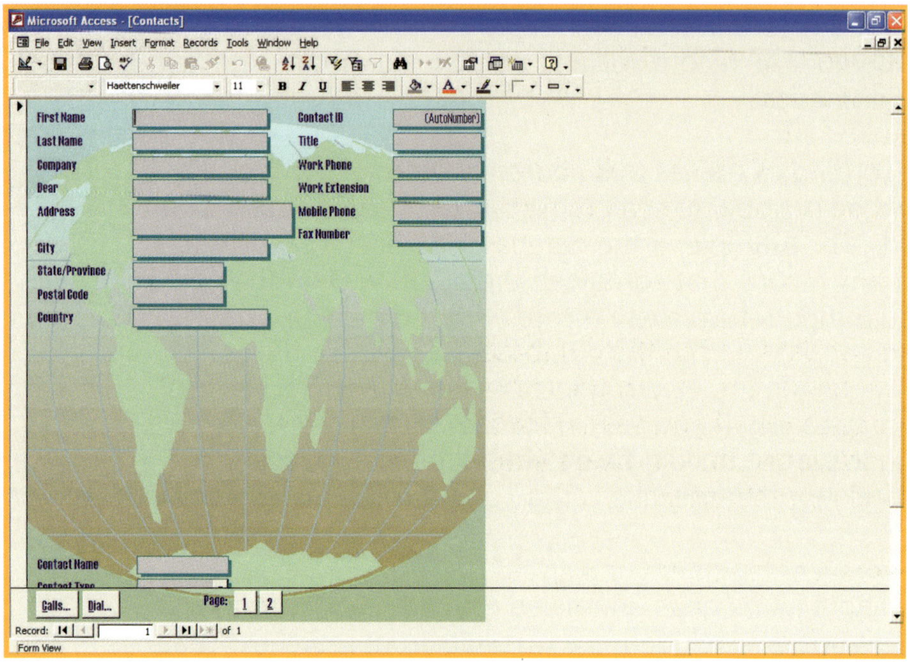

Data entry form

The entry of data can also be made easier by careful design of the **user interface** – the data entry form. This is the part of the database that can be easily overlooked, especially if the database is not going to be populated by the designer. The person who will be entering all the data is rarely asked for their input into the design procedure.

One long column

- Clear representation of the fields
- Easy to see when a field is empty
- Easy to read

A nested or justified arrangement

- Takes up less space on the screen
- Can be more difficult to read

Many websites have data entry screens that have been very carefully designed, taking into account the **ergonomics** and other factors that influence design. Unfortunately, some website designers are not so thoughtful!

Querying your data

All database applications allow you to carry out some form of interrogation of the data – a *query*. In the address book scenario, this would be a method of finding a particular entry. For example, suppose the data shown in the database discussed above is contained in the database. Each record is a self-contained set of data, but the software can look into it to find what data is contained within it. This means that the software can identify each field.

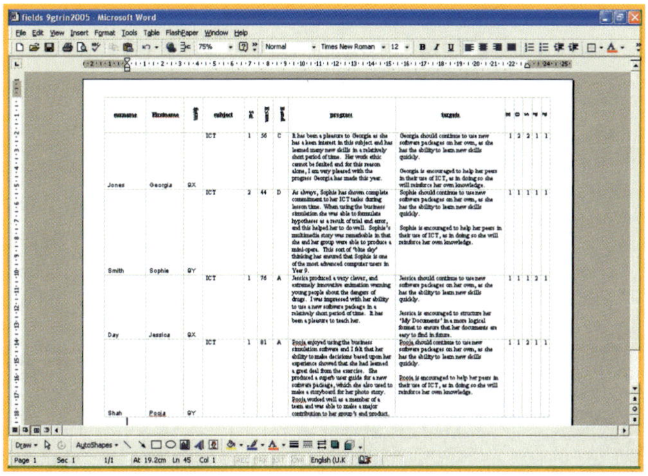

So if you ask the correct question you can find the correct data entry!

To find Amy's email address, you must ask the software to find any data record that has the three letters 'a', 'm' and 'y', arranged in the order 'amy', stored in the field 'First name'. Having found that there is an entry that matches the request, the next stage is to find the field 'Email address' in the record that matches the request, and show the user what is stored in that field. In this case:

amy@brireton.co.uk

As there are some duplicated sets of data within the database it is possible that a more complicated query would be needed to return the correct data – which is why it is so important to ask the correct question. If you search for the postcode for someone with the second name 'Williams', the software would return two postcodes. So how can you know which is the correct entry?

To seek this information the query must have two descriptors. Any of the following would work in this case:

Second name	First name
	Initial
	Street name
	Phone number
	Mobile number

So the query to find Ben Williams' postcode could be: Report the data entered in the Postcode field for any record that has 'Williams' stored in the Second name field and has 'B' in the Initial field.

In database language it is a bit simpler:
If Second name = 'Williams' + Initial = 'B' then Postcode

Reports

If the result from a query is only to be shown on-screen, and there is only one result, then the automatic display functions within the database application will be fine. But most databases store a lot more than 13 names and addresses!

Most database applications have some sort of reporting function – this is a section of the software that will display the results from a query and can be used to format data ready for printing. The report is usually generated from a set of data and cannot be amended, so if the report does not contain the correct data set, it is because the wrong question was asked!

This format of the report is usually suitable for inclusion in a document, just as it is. However, there are many other ways of displaying the information. The database application will have a variety of presentation themes, or layouts, for you to experiment with.

Merging data

Rather than include a report from a database in a document, it is possible to 'merge' the data from the database into another document. This process can use all or part of the database, and inserts the data into particular points of another document using 'merge fields'.

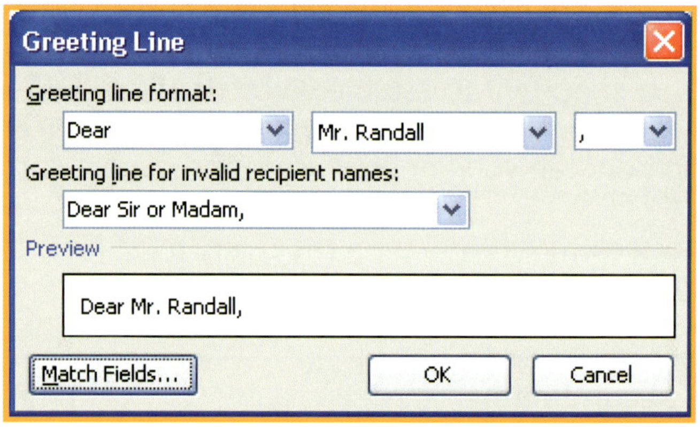

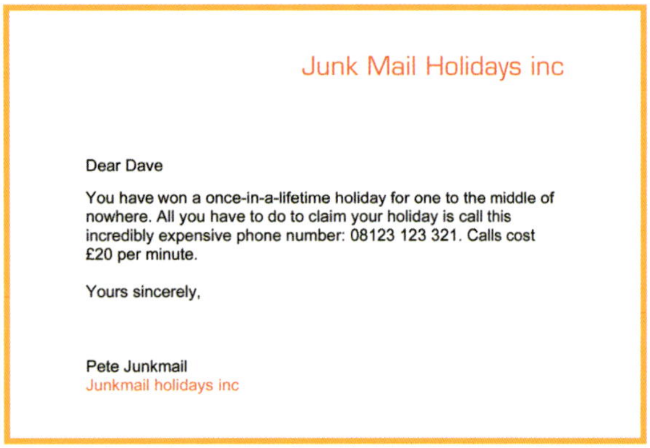

Mail merge is the most common operation for this, where a text document is set up and a linked database is used to supply names, addresses or other data to complete the document. This means that a standard document can be generated and then the mail merge fills in individuals' details. This lets you send a letter to any number of people, each one of whom thinks it was written specifically to them! (See Chapter 19.)

Homework

1 Build the database described in this chapter and add the data. Then use that data to carry out a mail merge to produce a short letter to be sent to everyone in the address book. Before you add any data to the database make sure that you have people's permission. Storing personal data on a computer can come under the Data Protection Act – there is more information on this and other legislation later.

2 Design and build a database to store the information you collected from the survey in Chapter 2. Remember to be careful to separate fields and match the data format before you import the data.

3 Investigate the querying and reporting functions of your database application. Produce examples of a successful query in a report format.

CHAPTER 4

Working with information

What you will learn in this chapter

You will learn how to write up the information you have collected and to combine it with images. You will learn how to make a website attractive to your target audience.

When you have researched your subject thoroughly you should have a good selection of information in the form of images, photos, clip art, surveys, sounds, movies and much more. So what are you going to do with all this information and how can you present it? Remember, it needs to be:

- Interesting
- Easy to follow
- Pleasing to look at
- Accurate

There is little point in gathering information for a project, then finding people will not read it either because it is not easy to read, or because its layout is so poor it looks bad!

Summarising information

When you write make sure you consider how your material could catch the eye:

- Write an unusual piece.
- Include new angles that make your work stand out from the rest.

- If possible, find out about the audience of the magazine, website or newspaper you intend to produce.
- Try to keep your writing up to date and be truthful.
- Look at the information from your surveys and present these to your audience in a way that makes the information understandable and interesting.
- Enticing headlines which summarise the material that follows are a great way to convey a message, as they get the reader interested.
- Follow a problem/solution format in your writing – asking a question and then suggesting a possible solution. (Also try comparing and contrasting ideas.)

Summing up information is best presented in the form of an inverted pyramid. This means that the first part of your work should be the key information. Answer the primary questions first, making sure to include any vital 'who, what, where, when, why and how' elements. Go straight to the point at the beginning because hopefully you will have time to explain details in subsequent paragraphs – but only if you grab the interest of the audience in the first few sentences.

The last section should include information that closes your work in a smooth but strong way. Do not leave people hanging, but on the other hand, do not drone on and on.

Conveying a message

If you try to mislead your audience it will backfire. You need to gain trust, so keep your information factual.

Information that is seen by the general public can influence them to be:

- Healthier
- Safer
- Cleaner
- Environmentally sound
- Wiser
- More secure
- More knowledgeable

Tip

Images

You may want to include photos, diagrams and sketches. Make sure that they are your own or that you have express permission to use them. Make sure that they relate directly to what you are promoting. Include both black and white and colour and a variety of sizes. Magazines and newspapers have varying requirements.

Persuading and convincing

Some messages may have more sinister motives behind them than others, but the power of printed material, broadcast sound, Internet sites or moving images to influence is very strong. Propaganda was used in the Second World War to influence people and help countries to win. Propaganda could be in the form of radio (sound), film (vision) or printed materials (posters, leaflets). Propaganda could lower or raise morale by telling lies or distorting the truth so the reader would be influenced by the information.

Propaganda was as strong a weapon as the bombs that were dropped and could easily make people give up hope or carry out certain actions. The leaflets dropped would often have strong images, with well-written, short, punchy text, designed to influence the reader.

Combining information

Tip

Sending and receiving information

You may be getting information or sending information via email. **Do not assume that everyone wants an email**. Though it might seem to be the easiest way to send or get information, take the time to develop separate contact lists for those who prefer email. Remember that a conventional letter or the phone may sometimes work better.

Most of the things we read or look at are a combination of pictures and words (books, magazines). Some work is presented with text and moving images and sound, such as films, TV, videos, DVDs, etc.). Sometimes it can involve all these methods or only some (the Internet or web pages, CDs or software). The information is blended together and presented to us in such a way that it is easy to follow and interesting to look at. It should also of course inform (allow you to learn from it). Sometimes you may gather vast amounts of information that needs to be sorted out in order for it to make sense to the reader or viewer. Computers are really good at doing just that; in Microsoft *Word*® you can write text, make forms or tables, include images, photos or even movies. In Microsoft *PowerPoint*® presentation software you can present information in the form of a slide show. Microsoft *Publisher*® is designed to let you present your information in the form of a book or magazine. Microsoft *Excel*® will allow you to print information in a systematic way and is great for dealing with numbers and data from surveys, making graphs and even including images.

Using design to convey your message

Designers are experts at conveying messages for their clients. Once they have their brief they should know the market they are targeting, the price of the products and what their intended market likes in the way of colours, styles, image and typography (the layout of text). If you go down the escalators in to the tube London , or in any big city, or look at advertisements on moving vehicles, you can see the designers have thought very carefully about the environment in which the information they are displaying is set. These methods of presentation require the minimum of text and the maximum impact, achieved by using big text, big images or contrasting or bright colours. What they do not do is put loads of information on the advertisements, because no one can read or absorb a lot of information in the few seconds they have to look at them. Often on tube escalators the message is repeated over and over as you only have a second to two to read them and too much information is impossible to take in!

> **Tip**
>
> A famous designer who specialised in layout once said, 'we are all lazy, if it's too difficult to read we don't bother'.

Attracting attention

Attracting attention to your message or information is not always about filling a page, be it a web page or a word-processed page, with information. Designers use space around images and text to draw in the eye. They use space between lines called *leading* (you find this in the Microsoft *Word* ® program under Format > Paragraph > Line spacing). It is called leading because for hundreds of years, right up until about 30 years ago, printers used lead strips to space out the lines of text.

You can also use bullet points

- like this to list or summarise information,

put boxes around text | like this |

change the colour

and e x p a n d text (Format > Font > Character spacing).

Target audiences

Audience is another word for your market, the people you are aiming your work at. Markets are dealt with in various parts of this book and more so in the fourth book of the series. Companies would often know more about the market than anything else before they decide to launch a new product. This is all done long before the product is available to the general public.

In order to know their market, companies build up a very accurate profile of their potential customers or audience. They will build up *visual images* of their customers:

- Homes and lifestyles
- Where they eat
- What they wear
- What music they like
- What they have in their homes
- Their cars
- Their holidays
- Their gardens
- Their toiletries

in fact, just about any information that would help them make a good decision about their product (product can mean anything from a tube of toothpaste to a website). The visual images are then put on a *mood board*. This is a board with a wide range of images. The designers will refer to it when making decisions based on the information.

What are the needs of your target audience?

The following people may need *special attention*:

- Children
- Babies
- Partially sighted people
- Poor readers
- Readers of other languages
- Colour-blind people
- People with learning difficulties

If you spend time getting to know your market you will soon have a good plan. Find out where your market lives, works and plays. Information about their interests or priorities is also helpful. Current markets will be similar to future markets, so if you get to know them, you will have a better idea of your target audience. This audience should be kept in mind at all times when developing an effective marketing strategy.

There are various ways to learn about who your market is and why they choose your presentation or information to read. Talk to them directly when possible. Try asking people for information while they are resting or at ease so you do not catch them at a bad time. It is easy to gather information when people feel respected, so avoid being bothersome.

People are often reluctant to give out information about themselves. Many companies have destroyed their customers' trust by selling personal information without permission. Be prepared to get mixed reactions when you ask questions, and do not get discouraged if people will not even tell you where they live. Inform people that you want to gain new information and that you need their help to establish a target audience.

Information for the Internet

It is also important to know who uses the Internet. The group of people who have access to the Internet is becoming larger and more diverse, but general demographic information provides insight into the future. Most people online are between 18 and 50 years of age. However, the 50-and-over group is growing more rapidly than any other. People use the Internet mainly for business, but product research and shopping are common reasons for personal use.

Demographics
The study of the human population's characteristics, like numbers, age, gender

Conveying a message

The Internet has opened up the world to many businesses that previously could not hope to find buyers for their products. Easy access via the Internet saves time, travel and printing costs. Having a web page means businesses can have online catalogues and images of their products that can be viewed from anywhere in the world.

This means that in order to communicate with the many cultures across the world you have to understand the particular needs of each one. Some websites are fine in plain English, but if you wish to communicate with a range of, say, Far Eastern countries, you need to make a version available in each particular language. Often it is only the text that needs to change while the graphics could well be identical. However, this will not always be the case, as some cultures will require images appropriate to their religion and beliefs. So, when designing, bear in mind who is going to read your work and make it appropriate to the people you intend to reach.

Targeting to convey your message

Marketing should be a focused process, and it is not easy. You need to break down your target audience and create smaller segments or target groups. Your work will vary depending on each individual group's characteristics and interests – you will want to accommodate everyone with appropriate text and graphics that they understand. If you sell a product, find a way to make that product appeal to different groups, with information addressing their unique needs. For example, B2B (business to business) target groups need more information and less 'fluff'. Learn how to make your message clear.

If you want to know more about the different target groups that are used by marketing organisations, go to http://www.businessbureau-uk.co.uk/sales-marketing/segmentation.htm

Language

Computers and the Internet give you the ability to reach just about any audience. Whether you decide to keep your business in Manchester or make it available in every city, people can access your site whatever their location.

Because you have the opportunity to reach people all over the world, you need to communicate your information particularly effectively. A wide range of customers means a wide range of needs, especially when it comes to language. Be open-minded about who you are designing for. Remember, not everyone speaks or reads English. If you are appealing to an overseas market, you may need a bilingual site, or you may need to provide several language options for your site's material.

Talk to people in their native languages or at a level they will understand. Children need a different vocabulary to adults, and teenagers may want different phrases and vocabulary too. The most common languages among the non-English-speaking population are Spanish, Chinese, German and Japanese. When and if you decide to go bilingual with your site, you need to make each new language section appear the same as the English section. The content, graphics and layout should be identical, or at least similar.

How interested will people be?

There are loads of websites and new magazines popping up today. Many of these fail because of weak marketing (gathering and using information on who will be looking at your work).

Presenting information is different on the Internet because it is fast-paced. Just as quickly as you attract a visitor to your website, you can lose a potential customer. When people watch TV or listen to the radio, they are often engaged in another activity, so their reaction time is slower. Because the Internet is interactive, hopefully people are paying attention to what is happening on-screen. If you decide to design a website, make sure you grab their attention quickly. Is the information presented so that it is exciting?

Fast-moving presentation or web pages save the readers time. Assume that most audiences lack the fastest modems and newest computers. Cut back on slow-loading features and use graphics sparingly. Time is precious on the Internet, so use it wisely. You have only seconds to interest someone and keep them coming back for more. The same is true of most information that is offered to the general public. If it is too difficult to follow because it is badly laid out, it will not be read or looked at.

Tip

There is more information about this in other chapters, particularly Chapter 18, Website software.

Making it happen

You are going to need a plan if you want to succeed. Decide how you want to publish your information. Consider how much time you are willing to spend on the activity, then brainstorm ideas on paper. Short-term plans help you stay on-task and keep you confident about your goals. Actively discuss these plans with others, and consider marketing techniques for the product or service you offer.

What to have in writing

- A mission statement for your publication (purpose of the site or document)
- Defined groups for your target audience and the best ways to reach them
- Goals for the product
- Ways to ensure success
- A plan with deadlines

Try newspapers, magazines, radio, TV and other media to find out what opportunities you may have for attracting the audience.

Checking your success

If you decide to produce a website you can check up on who is using it by using site analysis software programs, for example:

- www.webtrends.com
- www.netgen.com
- www.accesswatch.com
- www.statcounter.com

Services include daily, weekly or monthly reports for site information. You can customise your reports to include specific details, such as **demographic** information for your audience, **keywords** people use for your site and number of visitors per day. Depending on the service you use, this information is available for a small fee each month.

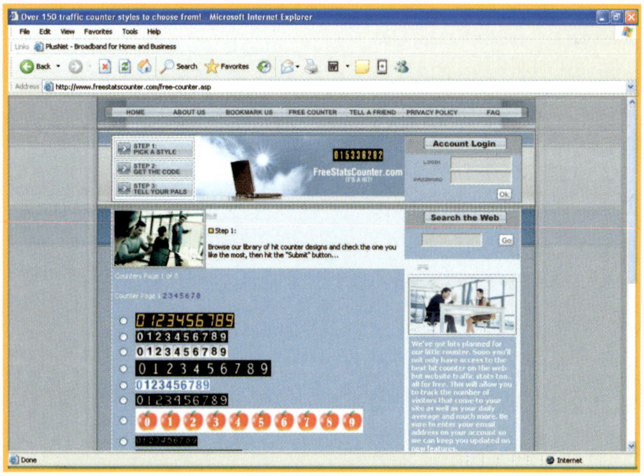

Even though people may look at your pages on a computer, they may not read them! If your information gets a mixed response, you will know you need to make some changes.

Check out similar sites or publications

If they are doing well, they must be doing something right! Find out about similar publications. Examine the graphics they use as well as their advertisement designs. Do not copy anything you see, but rather compare your work to theirs to see what is missing. Their site and location tell you a lot about the audience they appeal to. Is your target audience the same? Should it be?

Look to leading companies for clues. Successful companies outside of education can teach you valuable lessons about maintaining publications. Look in newspapers, Internet magazines and other sources to find the top 10 successful websites. Go on the Internet to see each one. Most newspapers are on the Internet each day. How do the paper-based and online versions differ?

Homework

1 Look at some text in magazine advertisements. Cut them out and write a short report.

Is it:

- Funny?
- Convincing?
- Informative?
- Exciting?

Who is the writer aiming it at? What makes you think this?

2 Look through some magazines. Find a full-page advertisement and look at the layout of the text, where it is placed, what font is used, how the lines are spaced, what colour the text is. Do the images and the text work with each other? Write a report on three different advertisements. Scan them and produce an A4 sheet, highlighting the good/bad points.

3 Try putting together a simple presentation, such as a few slides about your favourite hobby or pastime. Try to include a variety of elements: images, text, numerical data and graphs. Present it using two different applications: a paper-based system, such as Microsoft *Publisher*®, and an on-screen system, such as Microsoft PowerPoint® presentation graphics program. Present the two outcomes to others and ask them to comment on which they think is the most appropriate.

4 Select a fruit and find out about the nutritional value of the particular fruit. Try to write an advertisement that would appear in a newspaper to convince people that eating the fruit would be of benefit to them.

5 Select an everyday object, such as a pencil or pen, and research its history – when it was first developed, by whom, and so on. Try to inform your reader, in 100 words, about the details of its development and any other useful facts.

CHAPTER 5

Presenting information

What you will learn in this chapter

You will learn how to present your information in a way that is readable, attractive and fit for purpose.

Now you have all your information you need to spend some time sorting it out, deciding what is relevant and what is not. You may find some areas are strong and others weak on information. The latter would need further research. When this has all been done, you need to decide how to present the information to the viewer, listener or reader. This may be one of the most important decisions you make and it really needs to be right.

What do you want to do with your information?

- Do you want to change or influence people with your ideas?
- Do you want to educate them?
- Do you want to inform them?

Are you aiming your work at experts, beginners or does it have general interest? And how can you get them to read or look at what you have done? Hopefully the information below will help!

Fonts

Most people find that serifed typefaces are easiest to read on paper. Serifs are the little flicks on the top and bottom of typefaces such as Times. These are supposed to help the eye to follow the line of text. Sans serif typefaces work better on computers because the definition (quality of the image) is not so good. Avoid script typefaces, such as that shown below.

Edwardian Script is difficult to read but brilliant for wedding invitations.

You should personalise your work: try using fonts other than the **default** font. A lot of do-it-yourself web pages still use Times New Roman as the default font. Your pages will look more polished and professional and as a result will be easier to read if you choose the right font.

Pay attention to font size as well. If the text is too small, it is hard to read – that is pretty obvious. But large type can also be distracting, as a person with normal (or corrected) vision will have a hard time adjusting to the larger-sized font. For text, stick to a font size of 12 to 14 points.

The colour of the text is also important. Black on white is easiest to read when travelling, for example on the train, reading a newspaper or paperback. Outdoor road signs, especially on motorways, are often blue and white, which seems to be the clearest combination in a good range of lighting conditions.

The space between the lines of text, or leading, is also important – see page 38.

Software

The choice of software is getting bigger all the time. You probably have some or all of the applications listed in Table 5.1. The list contains the application name and the most appropriate use for the software.

Table 5.1

Application	Uses
Microsoft *Word* ® word-processing application	reports, papers, tables, brochures, letters, diary, creative pieces – poems, fables, fairy tales, lyrics, inspiration, graphic organiser
Microsoft *Powerpoint* ® presentation graphics program	oral presentations with accompanying visuals, overhead transparencies, charts
Microsoft *Publisher* ® desktop publishing program	brochures, newsletters, flyers

Microsoft *FrontPage* ® website creation and management tool	websites, multimedia projects, videos, maps, posters, oral projects
Adobe *Photoshop* ® image-editing software	altering images, posters, typography, web design
Adobe *Illustrator* ® graphics software	graphic design, text images, painting, drawing, technical illustrations
Zara	graphics, images, text typography
Microsoft *Excel* ® spreadsheet program	graphics, charts, tables, images and text plus charts
Macromedia *Dreamweaver* ® web design software	website design

Readability

It would be a shame if you have spent hours searching for information to present it to people in such a way that is unreadable or too confusing to follow.

There are some simple rules:

- Lay out text and images for your targeted market or audience.
- Make sure it is easy to read the text; fiddly text or too many fonts do not make for easy reading.
- Headings and titles can be fun and colourful, but still need to be read.
- Think about the age of your readers: if they are small children they will need simpler words than older ones. Think about the eyesight of your audience: older people may have visual impairment. The age of the reader may help with decisions on font style, colours and images.

Using space

Pages are used to pass on information. Sometimes we use words, sometimes we use images and sometimes we use a combination of both. If you use too many words, the reader may lose interest or get lost and move on. The golden rule is not to cover the page from top to bottom with text. Instead, use blocks of text that the

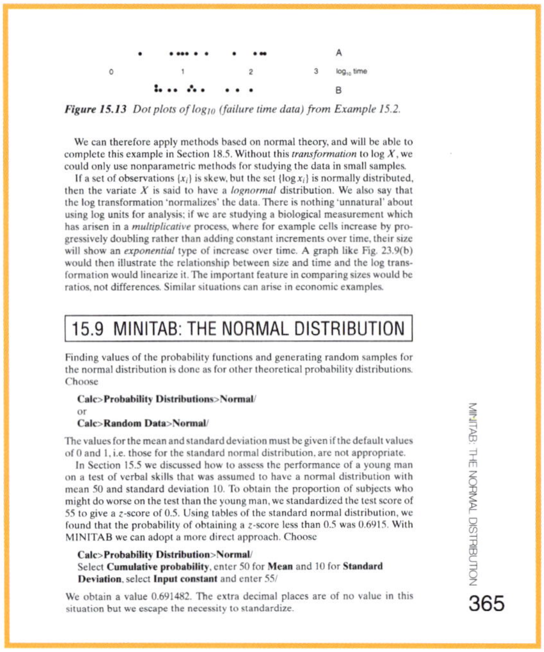

Figure 15.13 Dot plots of $\log_{10}$ (failure time data) from Example 15.2.

We can therefore apply methods based on normal theory, and will be able to complete this example in Section 18.5. Without this *transformation* to log X, we could only use nonparametric methods for studying the data in small samples.

If a set of observations $\{x_i\}$ is skew, but the set $\{\log x_i\}$ is normally distributed, then the variate X is said to have a *lognormal* distribution. We also say that the log transformation 'normalizes' the data. There is nothing 'unnatural' about using log units for analysis; if we are studying a biological measurement which has arisen in a *multiplicative* process, where for example cells increase by progressively doubling rather than adding constant increments over time, their size will show an *exponential* type of increase over time. A graph like Fig. 23.9(b) would then illustrate the relationship between size and time and the log transformation would linearize it. The important feature in comparing sizes would be ratios, not differences. Similar situations can arise in economic examples.

15.9 MINITAB: THE NORMAL DISTRIBUTION

Finding values of the probability functions and generating random samples for the normal distribution is done as for other theoretical probability distributions. Choose

Calc>Probability Distributions>Normal/
or
Calc>Random Data>Normal/

The values for the mean and standard deviation must be given if the default values of 0 and 1, i.e. those for the standard normal distribution, are not appropriate.

In Section 15.5 we discussed how to assess the performance of a young man on a test of verbal skills that was assumed to have a normal distribution with mean 50 and standard deviation 10. To obtain the proportion of subjects who might do worse on the test than the young man, we standardized the test score of 55 to give a z-score of 0.5. Using tables of the standard normal distribution, we found that the probability of obtaining a z-score less than 0.5 was 0.6915. With MINITAB we can adopt a more direct approach. Choose

Calc>Probability Distribution>Normal/
Select **Cumulative probability**, enter 50 for **Mean** and 10 for **Standard Deviation**, select **Input constant** and enter 55/

We obtain a value 0.691482. The extra decimal places are of no value in this situation but we escape the necessity to standardize.

MINITAB: THE NORMAL DISTRIBUTION 365

reader can cope with easily. Even books that are full of text use subtitles, **drop capitals**, margins, bullet points, and so on, to break up the mass of words.

Using bold or italics to emphasise a point is a trick commonly used when laying out text and letters. Underlining text usually makes it more difficult to read, so avoid this method. You need to make your pages reader-friendly so that people will enjoy reading the text all the way to the end.

Not many people will spend a long time reading long blocks of information unless they really have to. Some people prefer to print out blocks of information from the Internet because they find it easier to read on paper. A print-friendly version may encourage people to do this and is environmentally and economically friendly. Selected blocks of information work well on the web. Web browsers expect to find small blocks of text rather than loads of text to read.

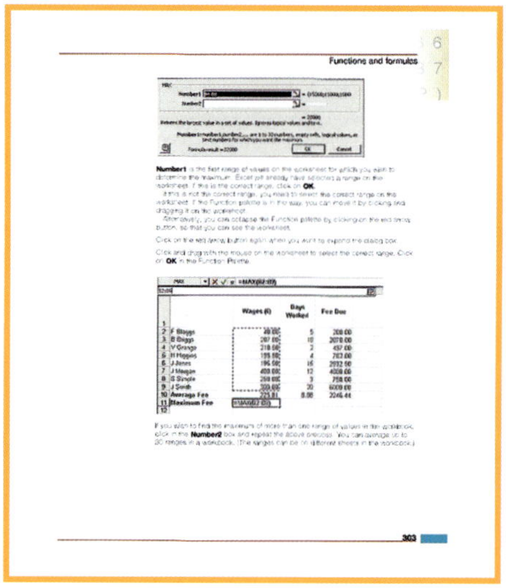

Functions and formulas

303

Tip

Practise breaking down large blocks of information into a quarter of the original content.

Blocks of text can also help you present and place information in a **house style**, so that people will get used to the way you lay out the pages and become familiar with the plan for the text.

Web pages are different to printed sheets. The screen is illuminated from behind the **pixels** and cannot currently produce as sharp an image or text as printed paper material can. The main advantages of the Internet are that it is flexible, fast and easy to find what you need, compared to browsing through magazines or specialist books. You do not need to find an index on the web, you simply search for the specific information you need.

Writing style

Blocks of information

Long before the world wide web was invented, writers discovered that readers appreciate short chunks of information that can be located and scanned through quickly. This method of presenting information translates well to newspapers, magazines and the Internet for several reasons:

- Few people spend time reading long passages of information unless they are really interested or really need the information. Most users either save long documents to disk or print them for more comfortable reading.
- Discrete chunks of information lend themselves to **web links**. The user of a web link usually expects to find a specific unit of relevant information, not a book's worth of general content. One to two pages (as printed) of information are about the maximum size for a discrete chunk of information on the web.
- Chunking can help organise and present information in a uniform format. This allows users not only to apply past experience with a publication to future searches and explorations, but also to predict how an unfamiliar section of a publication will be organised.
- Concise chunks of information are better suited to the computer screen, which provides a limited view of long documents. Long web pages tend to disorient readers; they require users to **scroll** long distances and to remember what is off-screen.

Tip

People read websites differently to the way they read books or newspapers. Not only is the web interactive, but also when someone visits a website, they usually have a specific goal in mind, whereas people looking for reading material will browse or flip through magazines.

Colour

Colour affects us all. Colours can attract the eye to different parts of your information; colours can make something stand out and become clearer. Colour can also help with the image you want to present. Many companies use colours to make their

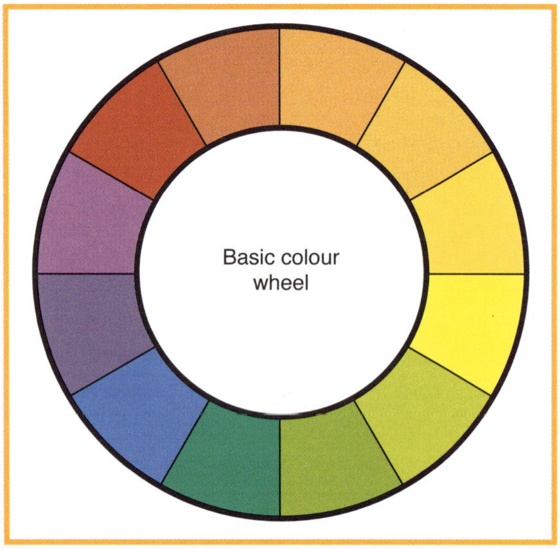

identity seem uniform. For example, DHL, the courier company, uses yellow and red on their vans, papers and websites; Shell Oil always uses yellow and red and always uses its logo in certain proportions, which are clearly spelt out in their trademark booklet. This makes a large company seem unified and allows people to recognise their products easily.

Colour schemes

Have you ever been unable to read the text because the font is not light enough to be seen on the dark background? Or, perhaps, the background is a bright colour and the white or black text seems to 'float' over the blinding background 'noise'. Think 'easy on the eyes'. Use neutral backgrounds (greys, blues, soft pinks or yellow) with a contrasting colour for text (darker shades of the background colour or black). For some reason, a lot of websites and presentations use black backgrounds with blue print! Try to avoid white text on a black background, as the text can appear to 'move'. Instead, use dark blue or another dark shade of a primary colour as a background with white text. It makes a big difference. Look at the page objectively. Maybe you can read the page, but can everyone else?

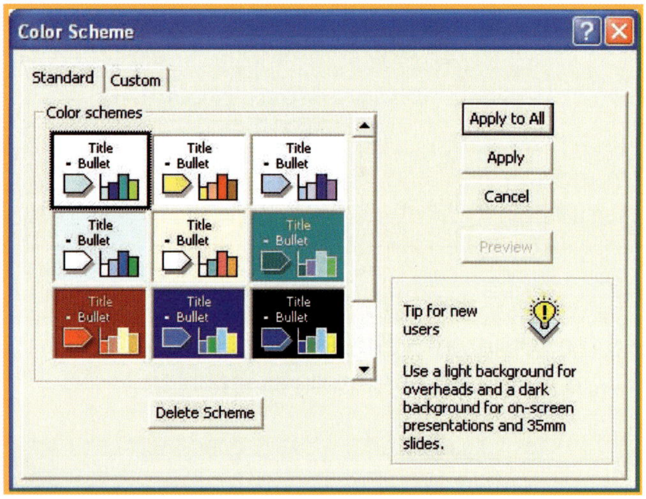

Layout

The top right of a newspaper page is usually the first part we look at, and the bottom left is usually the last part we look at. Advertising is more expensive to place on the right hand page and cheaper on the left-hand bottom of the page!

With the web, traditional viewing habits have changed. People tend to scan web pages looking for links or information that are of interest to them. For this reason you cannot assume people will start in the upper, left corner of the page and go left to the right, working their way down the page. A person's eyes will move around the page, stopping on graphics or text that are of interest. In some cases, things will draw their attention because of the content. In other instances, the placement, size or colour of an item will attract scrutiny.

Placing information

We all see things differently, so placing information is always tricky. Sometimes common sense will help you to make basic decisions. For instance, if the text is too small or is in the wrong font, it may not be easy to read, or the image may be inappropriate. These problems will quickly come to the fore and can be changed during testing. The problem with the Internet is that people will simply click away from the site. The problem with written information is that it can be quickly thrown away! We have all received flyers that go straight to the recycle bin. Information presented on the Internet should have content links on the top third of the page. These links need to be made really clear so that the reader knows what is **clickable** and what is **interactive**. Underline **hyperlink**s and make buttons look like they are just that! Create visual clues for your audience.

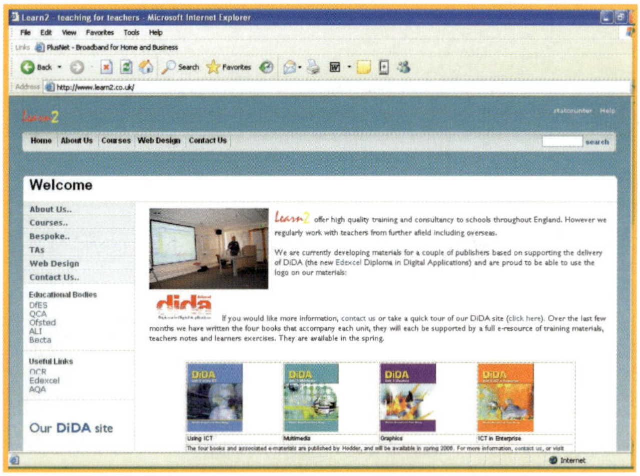

Keep text as snappy and short as possible, because people often scan-read pages! We do not necessarily look at every letter or word, so make sure it is easy to do just that. Probably the most powerful tool you have both on paper and on the web is space – if your main point is in a mass of space people just have to read it!

Design can be personal

What one person might love is what another person may hate. However, if you follow the rules we have already mentioned, you will get it about right for most people. Sometimes, however, a design style that breaks all the rules challenges what is a 'good' or 'bad' design. An early example of rule breaking was in the punk rock era, when graphics went crazy and what was once considered poor design fitted with the style of the music, fashion and the time.

Patterned backgrounds usually make reading and viewing difficult. Light text on very dark backgrounds is more difficult to read than dark text on light backgrounds, but not always. **Reversed text** is commonly used in small chunks. Reversing can make a title or subtitle stand out.

Mistakes, spelling and grammar

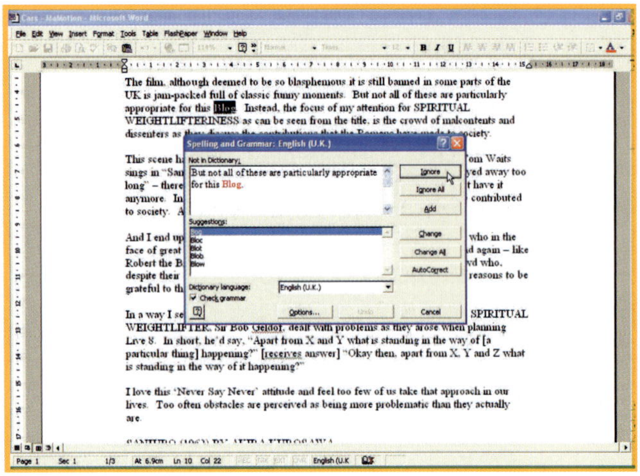

Spelling and grammar errors seem to jump right off the page, distracting the reader from the content. If you know that you have a problem in this area, *always* spellcheck. Copy your text into a Microsoft *Word*® document, spellcheck and then copy it back; no excuses. Of course, the spellcheck does not always catch words that are used incorrectly and often tries to substitute words that make no sense in context. **Read what you have written out loud**.

If you have difficulties, consider using help to write, or at least edit, your copy. The investment in time will be worth it in the long run.

Using music

Believe it or not, some people may not like your taste in music, so if you decide to add music to a web page or Microsoft *PowerPoint*® presentation, make sure it is appropriate! Try a site which has background audio playing. Do you like it? If you use music, make sure you offer your viewers the option of turning it off easily and quickly.

Summary

The golden rules for presenting your information are:

- Use a suitable typeface (font).
- Use the right size of text.
- Do not use too much text.
- Use images that have something to do with the text.
- Think carefully about the colours you use.
- Think about who you want to read the information.

Homework

1 Have a look at a range of typefaces and try them on-screen as small as you can. Which ones are easiest to read?

Produce a sample page in a range of different fonts and ask your classmates which they think is the best.

2 Take a fairly large advertisement from a magazine and try to make it suitable for placement on tube escalators or drive-by posters. Cut it down to a minimum to get the message across. This is a tricky task, but have a go.

CHAPTER 6

Paper publications

What you will learn in this chapter

You will learn how to format a word-processing document to produce a good effect when it is printed. You will also learn about using styles.

Paper publications are simply work that is done on a computer but designed to be printed on paper. (The chapter on word processing includes information on working with text and paper.) Nearly all printed matter these days is designed on computer, then either printed out on a local printer, printed out digitally by a specialist printer or sent to a print shop to be **litho** printed, the most common form of mass printing today.

Litho printing usually needs a printing plate with the computer-generated image burned onto it. Litho plates can be made of either thin aluminium or paper. Computers can transfer their data directly to a printing plate, which is then clipped on to the printing press.

Paper sizes

Work designed for printing is nearly always based on standard 'A' paper sizes.

Table 6.1 shows the width and height of all **ISO** A and B paper formats, as well as the ISO C envelope formats. The dimensions are in millimetres.

Table 6.1 ISO paper formats

A series formats		B series formats		C series formats	
4A0	1682 × 2378	–	–	–	–
2A0	1189 × 1682	–	–	–	–
A0	841 × 1189	B0	1000 × 1414	C0	917 × 1297
A1	594 × 841	B1	707 × 1000	C1	648 × 917
A2	420 × 594	B2	500 × 707	C2	458 × 648
A3	297 × 420	B3	353 × 500	C3	324 × 458
A4	210 × 297	B4	250 × 353	C4	229 × 324
A5	148 × 210	B5	176 × 250	C5	162 × 229
A6	105 × 148	B6	125 × 176	C6	114 × 162
A7	74 × 105	B7	88 × 125	C7	81 × 114
A8	52 × 74	B8	62 × 88	C8	57 × 81
A9	37 × 52	B9	44 × 62	C9	40 × 57
A10	26 × 37	B10	31 × 44	C10	28 × 40

How to change the paper size for a print job

You can change the paper size for a print job. This will allow you to print on paper of different sizes, including envelopes and index cards. These instructions should work for most Microsoft *Windows*® applications.

1. Open the File menu and click Print.
2. Click on Properties.
3. Click the Setting tab.
4. Click on Paper Size.

5 Select the size you want.

6 If you can't find the size you want, select Custom. A box will appear where you can enter your own sizes.

7 Click OK.

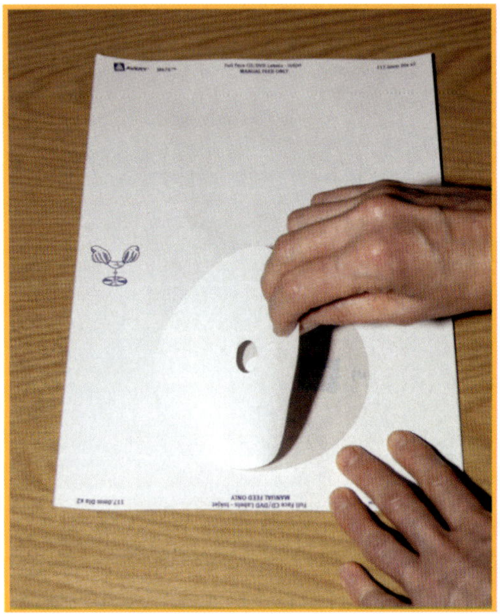

To ensure accurate, economical printing, when publications are designed or typeset it is important to set your computer to the 'A' sizes listed in Table 6.1. Selecting a standard size also helps your publication to have a consistent look or **house style** (see page 60).

If you want to print CD labels or odd shapes for a particular printout you can either download software that has what are called printing templates, or you can get software specifically designed for the job included. There are products with matching software applications that are designed to simplify the layout and printing of items such as business cards, brochures, postcards and labels for envelopes, CD-ROMs and floppy disks.

Not all printers will accommodate all sizes of paper. Your choices are limited to the sizes your printer can handle. The printers you work with are probably A4 or A3, the largest size commonly available. Your local print shop may print up to A1 size for you, but this could be expensive!

Page orientation

You can choose the page orientation from either landscape (the paper is wider than it is tall) or portrait (the paper is taller than it is wide – this is the usual orientation).

How to change the page orientation

1 Click the File menu, then Page Setup.

2 To print a document in landscape orientation, click the button beside 'landscape'.

3 To print a document in portrait orientation, click the button beside 'portrait.'

4 Click OK.

Landscape

Use landscape orientation to accommodate wide graphics or if you want to place graphics side by side. Choose your orientation as you compose the page, so you can see how the page will look as you create it. Not all printers will print in landscape orientation.

What to put in your printer

Check the specifications of the paper you buy to make sure you are getting the most out of your printer.

- Generally speaking, thicker paper produces a better quality final print, so use a lightweight paper if the quality of the print is not so important.
- On the other hand, use a thicker paper, 80 to 100 gsm, for a higher quality copy.
- Coated paper can be used for printing high quality graphics or images, as the coating stops the ink from being absorbed, which gives a sharper image.
- There are special coated papers available for printing photographs (e.g. from a digital camera).
- Use the unused side of scrap paper for very rough versions of documents.
- Chemically treated papers can be used to create your own transfers for T-shirts and fabrics!

Warning

- Never put anything plastic in your printer, especially a laser printer, as this could melt and ruin the machine.
- Never tug at the paper on slow full colour print runs; these may be slow, but tugging will result i white strips appearing on the finished print.
- Check that your printer accepts thicker paper before using card, as the rollers can be misaligned if the printer does not have the correct settings.

Deleting a print job

You can cancel or delete a print job if you decide that you do not want to print the document after all. You will save paper and reduce the wear and tear on your printer if you cancel unwanted jobs, especially if the document is several pages long. These instructions are for Microsoft *Windows*® operating systems. Instructions for other operating systems may vary.

How to cancel a print job

1. Click on the Start menu and then click on Settings.
2. Next click on Printers.
3. A window will appear. Click on the printer you are using. A window will appear listing all the print jobs that are waiting to print.

4 Select the document that you want to cancel.

5 Click on Cancel Printing. If the print job has already started, it should cancel when the current page finishes printing.

6 At step 5 you can choose to pause the print job.

Layout

Margins

When you start to design the layout of a paper publication you need to remember that most printers do not print to the edge of the page.

You cannot cancel someone else's print job, only your own.

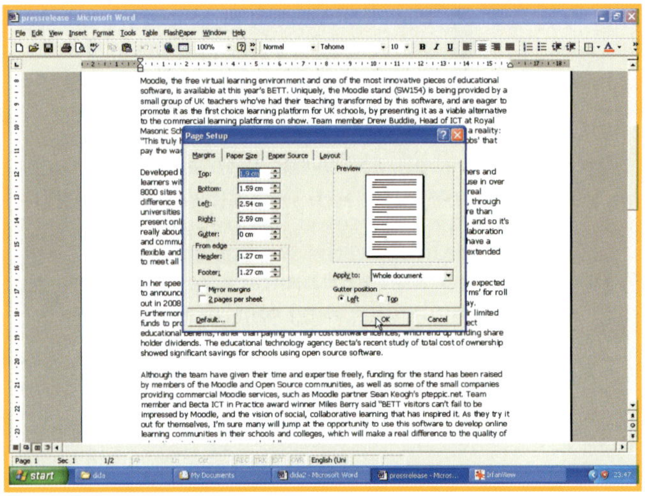

(Sometimes this looks good and professional designers often have work appearing to go off the edge of the page – this is called '**bleed**'). What you have to decide is what the margins around your work will be set to. Usually people just put up with what has been set (the default), but you can change the margins by going to File > Page Setup > Margins, and then turning the scroll arrows up or down to set them how you would like them to be.

Look at a newspaper and note the columns, then try copying the layout in your word processor or DTP application.

Columns

Columns are more important than most people realise, and they can be set easily in most word processors or desktop publishing software. The reason they are used is that they break up large blocks of text, thus making it easier to read. If you look at newspapers, you will see that they always have the text in columns because the lines are shorter. As many newspapers are read either on the move or fairly quickly, this helps the readability.

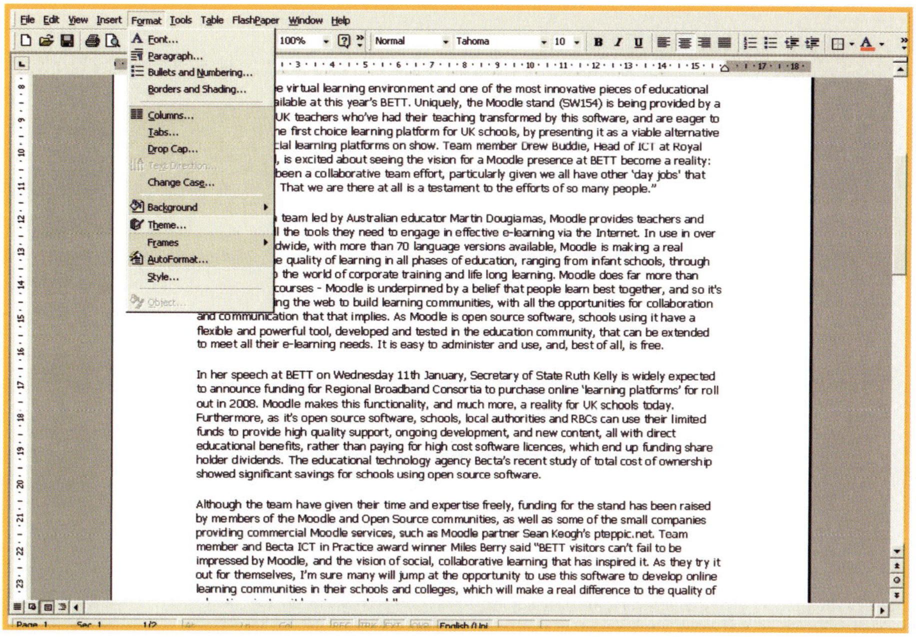

Columns can be set using Format > Columns. Here you can change the number of columns you want and the space between them, the '**gutter**'.

House styles

If brochures, leaflets and other publications are published as a range of items, they need to have a similar look so they appear to be part of a group of publications. Whether they are for internal company use or external readers, they need to meet the same standards.

A consistent style should be used for all stationery items and literature, with the identifier/logo/title appearing in the preferred position and main title positioned top left. Careful graphic design will give your publication a unique visual identity. A 'signature' graphic and page layout allows the reader to grasp immediately the purpose of the document and its relation to other pages. Graphics can also show that pages are linked in some way.

Headers and footers

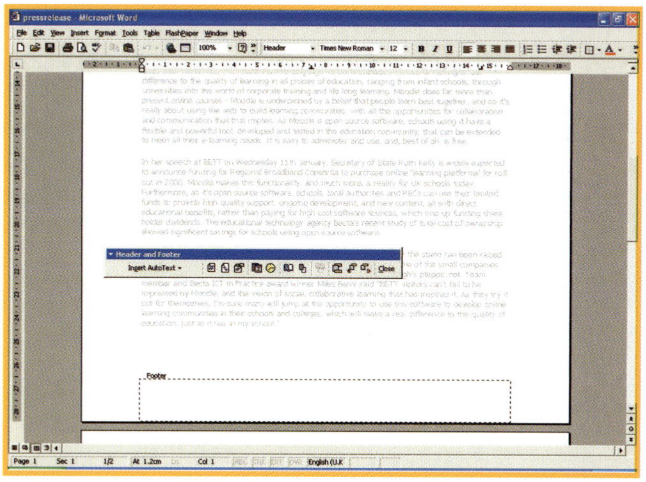

Headers and footers are text boxes that appear at the top and bottom of each page and they may or may not be needed. The same design can be used throughout your publication. Headers and footers could include your colour schemes, logo or an image or house style.

In Microsoft *Word* ® you find the header and footer option by clicking View, then Header and Footer. If you are in page or Print layout view, click the header and footer that appears as grey text. The header and footer toolbar should always then be present.

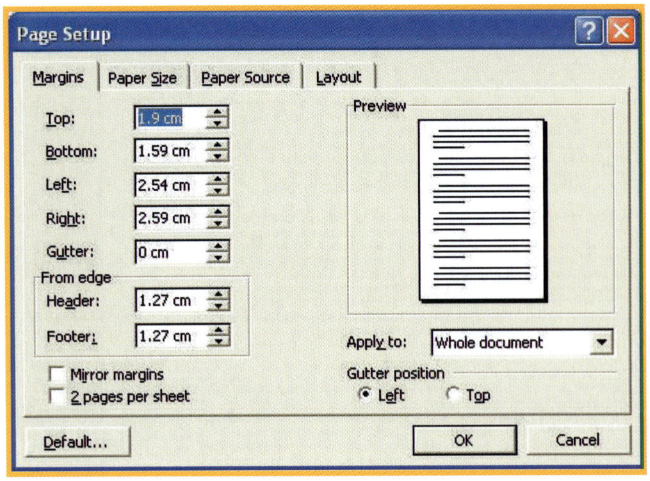

A different header and footer on the front page

1 Open your document as normal.

2 Click Page Setup on the File menu, then the Layout tab.

3 Click on Different first page under 'Headers and Footers.'

4 Click on OK.

5 Save the document.

Odds and evens

If you want to show your headers and footers differently you could try this option. Follow steps 1–2 above, then click Different odd and even.

Possible problems

- **I can't see the headers and footers.**

  Click the View menu. If you are in Normal view, it is necessary to click Header and footer.

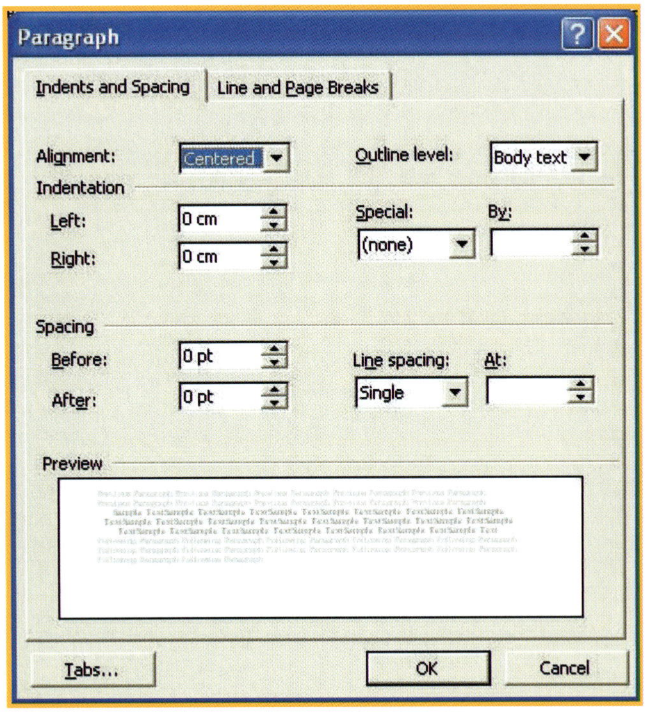

- **The section break doesn't allow me to have both portrait and landscape text on the same page.**

  Microsoft *Word* ® software will not allow you to do this by using a section break.

Tabs and indents

Tabs can be inserted manually and are used to show breaks in lines of text or to produce emphasis. Tabs can be set on the bar at the top of Microsoft *Word* ® or put in manually with the tab key, which is on the left of your keyboard, usually with two arrows pointing in different directions. Tabs and indents can be set in the Format menu, by clicking on the Paragraph option.

Styles

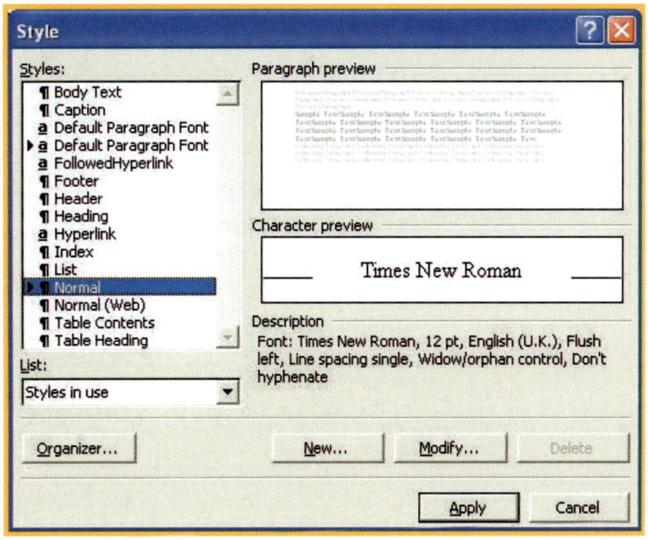

Styles are very important, but often overlooked. Styles can be a group of predefined formats, instructions on font style, size, colour, and so on. You can applying these to your work by simply highlighting and applying the formatting instructions. This saves you time, especially on large documents or a range of documents for which you have produced a house style. You can also apply styles quickly, changing normal text into the correct style for **footnotes**, **headlines** and **body text** (the main text style for the document). In the Style **dialogue box** you can set up your style, give it a sensible name, such as 'body text' or 'subtitles', and simply click and apply it. It is a bit like highlighting and changing a font, but adds many more features. Styles are time savers and are available in most word-processing and desktop publishing software packages.

Viewing styles

Styles can be seen in the formatting toolbar or from the Format menu, by clicking on Style. Some desktop publishing software has a similar feature and the style menu can be seen as an extra box on the screen at all times. For example, this feature is obviously useful when you are working on newspapers or a frequently published newsletter.

As many publications are made up from separate blocks of word-processed text which have been imported into a publication, styles soon become invaluable.

Tip

You can also press Ctrl+Shift+S and then click the up or down arrow keys on the keyboard to move through the list of available styles. Pressing F4 on the keyboard once inside the Style box activates the drop-down list, which you can then traverse with arrow keys.

Homework

1 Take a popular tabloid paper, such as the *Daily Mail* or *The Sun*, count how many columns the publication is based on, look at the text margins and general page layout. Try to identify the house style and make a list of what you find. Look for consistency across the pages. For example, are numbering, titles and subtitles the same style throughout the newspaper?

2 Copy a block of text into a Microsoft *Word®* document and try to make it more difficult to read and then easier. Can you improve upon its readability? Is it possible to make it unreadable (illegible)? What difference does a serif or sans serif font make to the ease of reading? Play around with the leading. Print some out and try testing your work on others.

3 Text boxes can be used to contain a section of text with or without a border. They are also moveable as independent blocks. Try moving a **text box** using the shaded edges. Then try inserting a text box into a block of text with a coloured background using the fill.

CHAPTER 7

On-screen publications

What you will learn in this chapter

You will learn the basics of producing a presentation for displaying on-screen.

The presentation of information is an important aspect of any ICT work, whether it is a simple poster advertising a social event or a multimedia extravaganza! Whatever it is that is being presented, the medium, the method of presentation, must be used to its full potential.

Chapter 6 dealt with paper-based work; this chapter is concerned with on-screen publications – materials that are designed to be presented on a screen.

The screen

Screens come in lots of different sizes and show different qualities of image – in a good design, these variations will all be taken into account.

The most common place for a publication to be presented is on a computer screen, or through a multimedia projector. Computer screens are classified by the number of pixels (abbreviation of 'picture cells') they can show – the **resolution**. The most common resolutions are:

640 × 480
800 × 600

1024 × 768
1152 × 864

Although this is usually related to the physical size of the screen – the larger screens usually have a higher resolution – it does not always follow. Some users set their screen to a particular resolution because they prefer the way it looks.

A resolution of $m \times n$ means that the screen can show a rectangle m pixels wide by n pixels high. Usually, the horizontal dimension (width) is the greater (most people, if asked, would prefer to look at a screen that is wider than it is tall) and preferably a 'golden rectangle'. However, these proportions do not match paper proportions, which can create problems.

Multimedia projectors and other devices run from a standard computer will normally run at the same resolution as the screen. There are now more computers with **widescreen** displays, which adds another set of variations, as they can be widescreen and run at different resolutions! This has led to a different method of measuring screens, as the ratio of width to height, for example, 4:3, 16:9, 16:10, 2:1.

To add even more complications there are also differences in the number of colours that can be displayed, from monochrome (black and white or green) to 16.7 million colours!

An on-screen presentation can be very different to an old-fashioned paper one like this

Because of the complexity of all these different screen sizes and resolutions, most on-screen publications are developed to be shown on an average system – something that shows 800 × 600 resolution with a fixed range of 256 colours. This has led to a common format for many publications, including multimedia presentations, websites and other on-screen publications.

Generally, on-screen publications are designed to be shown on a relatively low-resolution screen, so that users with older or less advanced machines can access the materials. This has become an important issue over recent years, as legislation has come into being regarding accessibility. It is now a legal requirement to ensure that any user, regardless of disability or other disadvantage, must be able to access materials. For more information, take a look at the legislation in Table 11.1, page 108.

Software

On-screen presentation systems, such as Microsoft *PowerPoint* ® software, have a vast array of templates and page layouts (**slides**) that can be used to quickly generate a professional-looking presentation. These are usually built to fill the screen. Although they can be adapted to an individual's needs or preferences, they all work on the basis that the screen they will be shown on is 4:3 with limited colours, usually 16. If a standard presentation is shown on a screen that is not 4:3, such as a widescreen, the images and text will appear distorted.

Presentation software is often used to illustrate information for an audience. It can be designed to be displayed on a small screen, projected on to a large screen, moved forward section by section by the operator, or left to run automatically. Systems that can be left to run a series of **slides** without interaction are often placed in public places, such as post offices, railway stations, libraries and shopping centres, where the public can watch the display, but have no control over its progression.

The other use for such software is to provide an interactive system for a particular user. This can be the author, perhaps a teacher presenting a series of slides on a topic they have written; or a viewer – someone watching a presentation on their own, perhaps over the Internet, that was written by someone else.

Recent developments in software means that presentation software can now include a whole range of different formats of data, for example:

- Text
- Images – **vector** or **bitmap**
- Sound – **MP3**, **WAV**
- Video – **Mpeg4**
- Animations – **swf**

Slides can also contain interactive components, such as **hotspot**s, buttons, forms and all manner of other bits and pieces. There are also *forward* and *back* buttons, so that the presenter (or viewer) can jump back and forth through the slides.

Themes and layouts

To make the job of the designer a little easier, the applications provide a range of themes. These determine the styles that the slide will display – the colour, size and font of the text, the background colour and style, and how the slide operates. As mentioned above, all these elements can be adjusted, but they do give a good starting point.

It is good practice to develop your own theme and apply it to a 'master slide'. This is a sort of template that can be applied to any slide – it can affect any part of the slide layout, and therefore gives a uniform appearance to a presentation.

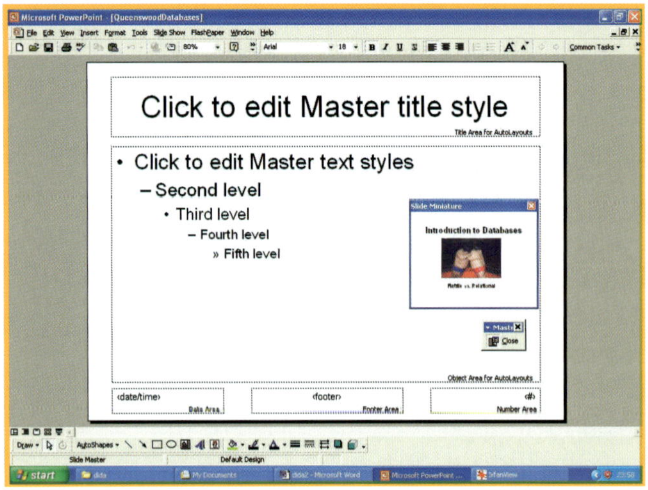

The page design is usually made up of an area for a heading (usually formatted to be in a large, easily read font) and a number of areas for other elements.

Because presentations are usually read from a screen, the slides should not contain much text – often just a few **bullet points**. The detail is often left for the speaker to explain. Again, like a teacher using a presentation, the slides are there to structure the lecture; the detail is in what the teacher says. As the presentation is usually run from a computer, it is possible to add hyperlinks to other documents or websites. These can then be opened when the link is clicked during the presentation.

As with paper publications, layout is very important. The page must be easy to understand and follow. This is particularly important when the information is new or complex, as the audience will have enough to concentrate on without getting confused by poor layout or hard-to-read text.

Each slide is a separate page, so the software usually has some trickery that can be added that allows the pages to 'turn' smoothly – this is called a **transition**. Some transitions are better than others, and indeed some of them can be very distracting. A simple fade in or out is usually best. Try to avoid using different transitions, as the audience will start to think about what the next transition will be, rather than listen to the speaker!

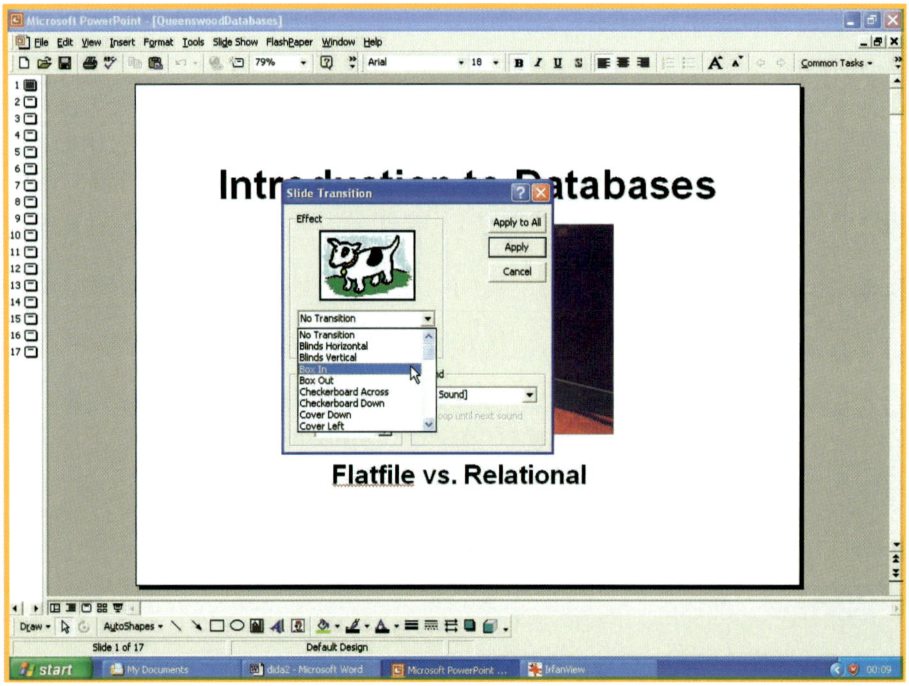

To make the presentation clear, there are a few simple rules to follow:

- Use high-contrast colour schemes: dark backgrounds and light-coloured text work well for on-screen publications; projected presentations may be better with a light background and darker text.

- Avoid too many different typefaces – limit yourself to three.
- Do not have text running from edge to edge or side to side: it is difficult to read, especially if it is displayed via a large projection system.
- Use bulleted lists rather than full sentences – the first time you have been told not to use good grammar! The presenter can add the detail.
- Use diagrams and charts to illustrate a point, but try to avoid too much frivolous imagery – it detracts from the message, as do animations or sound effects. These are great for fun, but should be avoided when doing a professional presentation.

A good presentation takes a lot of care and planning, as does a website or paper publication.

- Collect together the data/information you will be using, so that you can convey the necessary meaning.
- Produce any charts or graphs using compatible software (most standard packages can be included).
- Make sure any diagrams are suitable and will be legible when displayed on a screen.
- Decide on a theme or template, bearing in mind the rules mentioned above. You may have to develop your own, or use a **corporate** style.
- Plan the progression through the presentation – this can be done using **storyboard**s, **mind-mapping** software or other planning tools.
- Build the slides using the presentation **software**.
- Check the order – this can be done by simply reading the content – does it make sense?
- Proofread the text, checking for grammar, spelling and other text-based errors.
- Add any hyperlinks and check they are working.
- Test the presentation on the screen you intend to use – if the publication is to be delivered on a range of different machines, the presentation will need testing at different resolutions and screen sizes.
- Test the publication with a sample audience; this is only necessary for testing new templates or prior to the launch of an important product.

A similar procedure should be followed for a website or other publication that will be made available to others. However, each different format of publication will have its own particularly important aspects.

For websites and other publications to be delivered over the Internet it is important to keep the file size relatively small. Most people still access the Internet through a **dial-up** connection, meaning that downloading and displaying pages can take a long time – a 1 MB file can take over 10 minutes to download. An A4 image of acceptable quality could be well over 25 MB!

Website design tends to be more complicated than a presentation. The audience is much wider and the message needs to be more self-contained, as there is rarely an expert available to help explain the details. Where a presentation usually uses a theme and page layout, a website is often built using frames – each frame is, in effect, a separate page.

A slide-based presentation tends to be linear (slide 1, slide 2…), but a website can be navigated in different ways by each user – page 1, page 24, page 3, page 7, page 1… This is because websites are usually built with some sort of **navigation** bar or a set of links that the user clicks to move through the site. This system can be used in a slide-based presentation, but as the users tend to be led through the presentation, stage by stage, it is less often employed.

There is more detail on the intricacy of web design in Chapter 18.

Publication of the presentation

A publication to be distributed via email must not exceed 2 MB, as many email **servers** (the machines that transfer the emails around the Internet) do not accept files larger than 2 MB.

If particular colours or fonts have to be used – as in corporate publications – the **colour palette** and the font must also be sent, as there is no guarantee that the user's machine carries the same colours. One way of getting round this is to **embed** the font and colour palette, by converting the publication to a self-contained application – Microsoft *PowerPoint* ® presentation software can do this; other systems may not. Converting to **PDF** (**portable document format**) is usually a safe bet – but make sure it converts everything!

If the publication is to be viewed using the original application used to generate the presentation there are rarely serious problems, as the software has been specifically developed to carry out the task. However, if the publication is to be viewed through a third-party piece of software, as websites generally are, then there could be problems with the software itself. There are a number of different **browsers** (applications that convert web pages into a viewable page), the most common being the Microsoft *Internet Explorer* ® browser. Each application is slightly different, and therefore could make your publication appear different for different users.

If you carry out extensive testing across different machines, running different resolution screens and browsers, you should be able to iron out most of the potential problems.

Another potential problem is developing materials that are compliant with the Disability Discrimination Act and W3C guidelines (see www.w3.org). These are mentioned in greater detail later, but in developing an on-screen publication it is important that these are taken into account:

- Text must be clear and a standard screen reader, such as JAWS®, should be able to read it aloud.
- Images should have logical titles; web images should have **ALT tags**, giving information for screen readers.
- Navigation from page to page should be logical and straightforward.

When all these things have been taken into account, you should be well on your way to developing a professional publication. The main problem still not addressed is the content – but that is down to you!

Paper versions

The very nature of on-screen publishing means that the publication is not designed to be printed, but that does not mean that paper-based versions are not useful – or, in some cases, essential.

Multimedia presentation software will have a facility for printing the slides, in a range of formats, in both colour and monochrome:

- Full size – suitable for transferring to overhead transparencies (**OHTs**) for use on an overhead projector (**OHP**).
- **Handouts** – **thumbnails** of the slides, with space for note taking, usually distributed to the audience.
- **Outline text** only – useful for the speaker to keep as a reference so they know what is coming up.
- Speaker's notes – something which is often neglected, a more comprehensive set of notes. These can be used to help explain the content of the slide. There is space for the author to make extra notes, usually for their own benefit, but if the presentation is to be delivered by someone else these can be essential.

Websites are a little more difficult as the 'page' size is much more open to the designer's needs. If a printed version is required, again, it may be best to provide a PDF of the pages, as they can be set to a specific size, such as A4.

Chapter 16 on Presentation software will show you more detail regarding slide transitions, tables and backgrounds.

How to get good marks

- ✓ Make sure your slide presentations are easy to follow, both in terms of presentation and understanding. Complex slides full of animation may be fun, but they are not easy to follow.
- ✓ Think about your audience and present your on-screen presentation to them, not to yourself. Only by researching and getting the correct information is this possible.
- ✓ Presentations should, generally speaking, be no longer than 20 minutes. People lose concentration fairly quickly, as you probably know. So make it short, sharp and snappy – **SSS**.
- ✓ Learn to use your equipment, such as slide projectors.
- ✓ Have a presentation plan and make sure you know your subject.
- ✓ Present for your screen. Whether it is a web page or perhaps an interactive whiteboard, whatever it is the presentation design should suit the screen it is to be shown on.

Homework

1. Present a three-slide presentation, giving clear advice to others on how to give a professional on-screen presentation.
2. Convert the presentation to be suitable for viewing over the Internet.
3. Produce PDFs of the slides or pages, including speaker's notes.

CHAPTER 8

Creating an e-portfolio

What you will learn in this chapter

You will learn what you are expected to provide for assessment, and how to set about compiling your e-portfolio.

Your work will be assessed by your teacher, against a set of criteria from the subject specification. For your work to be assessed, you must submit a portfolio. Unlike most other subjects, for DiDA you *must* submit it electronically – an e-portfolio. You save all your work on a computer system and never need to print anything out.

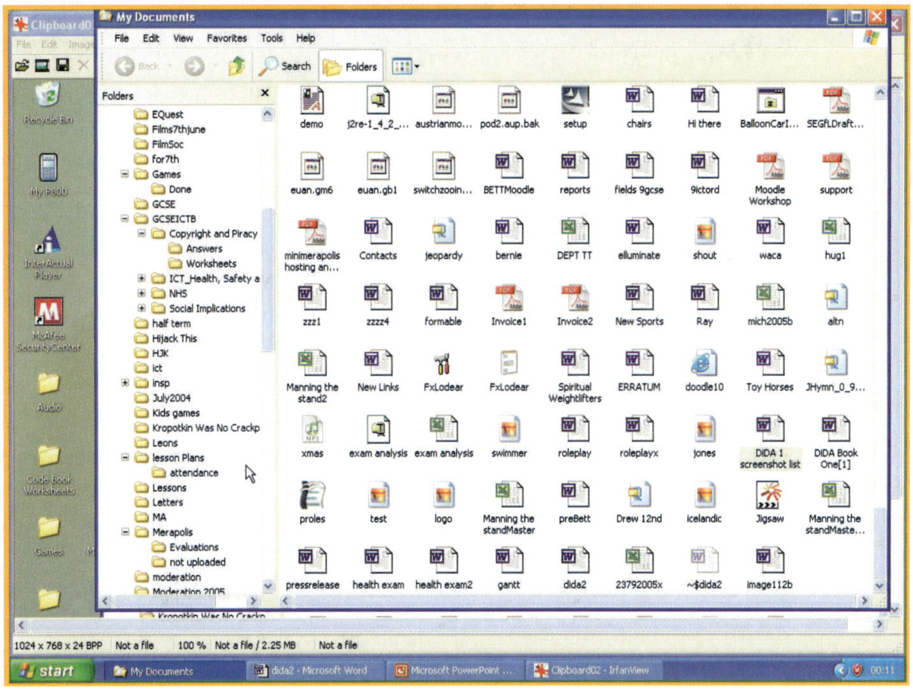

The e-portfolio must contain everything that you need to have assessed. If anything is not in it, it will not get marked, and you will not get the credit for it – you may even fail the course because of it. Before you start to compile your e-portfolio, you must ensure that you know exactly what you need to include. Your teacher will advise you on this. But you should also make sure you have looked through the guidance from Edexcel. The latest information will always be posted on their website:

www.edexcel.org.uk
http://dida.edexcel.org.uk/home/

You also need to make sure that you have a back-up of your work, saved securely away from the machine you normally work at. It could be on a CD-ROM: these cost very little and one can probably hold all your work. If you take a back-up copy home you will be able to find it again if you have a disaster at your college or school. However, you must remember that you are **not** allowed to work on your DiDA SPB at home. You may find that the original pieces of work are kept in your network area, and you use copies for the e-portfolio.

Navigation

When you are ready to start to build the e-portfolio you need to arrange it in such a way that your teacher and the moderator can find everything easily. This means that you may need to develop some sort of file structure, with a *contents* document with links showing where each piece of information can be found. Some of you may be given a file structure to work from.

Ideally, you will have a variety of documents or different files that are grouped together like a website. Each file is linked to a **home page** and can be accessed from there.

The home page

The main user interface of your e-portfolio will be the home page – so make it a good one! Try to make your home page as interesting and professional-looking as you can. Use all the tricks you have picked up through the course to impress your teacher and the moderator.

The home page should be of a standard file type, such as **html**, and will contain a number of important details, as well as carrying a short description of the files or documents:

Home page details:
Name
Candidate number
Centre number
Project title

Date of submission
Group name/Teacher name

Short description of what materials are available in the e-portfolio
Short description of each material, with a hyperlink to the file or document

A well-designed home page is a great advantage in your e-portfolio. You could build a **smart page**, with **rollover buttons** and interactive messages, or keep it plain and simple. Whatever you decide, you should introduce the reader to what they are about to see. Try welcoming the reader, as shown below.

Welcome to my e-portfolio. Over the past three months I have been working on a project, 'Producing material for the launch of a new restaurant'. The page links below will take you to a variety of documents, detailing the process I worked through and the outcomes I generated in trying to satisfy the various requirements of the project brief.

Although each link has been tested before submission, if anything does not work, each folder contains an index with a set of links to each file within the folder. If there are any further problems, you can email me at dave@e-portfolio.co.uk

You will be told what to include in the SPB. It may be something like this:

<button>Images – here you will find 10 images of materials I produced for this project.

1 a design for a logo (to appear on the headed notepaper and menus)
2 four versions of the headed paper and menu designs
3 a postcard to be sent to prospective customers
4 a poster to appear in a local public centre
5 a handout to be distributed in a shopping centre
6 an on-screen presentation

<button>Project Planning – here you will find my initial plan and time allocation record and the revised plan and project quality review record, and my diary.

1 Initial plan
2 Time sheet

3 Revised plan
4 Quality review record
5 Diary

<button>Information Sources – this folder contains three files: a list of my bookmarks, with short descriptions of each site, a detailed bibliography including all the magazines and books I have used, a list of images and image galleries I have visited in developing my work.

1 Bookmarks
2 Bibliography
3 Image library

<button>Data Manipulation – in developing my ideas, I carried out a variety of research, including a survey and two interviews. The results of this research is contained in these files.

1 Questionnaire
2 Results
3 Interview script
4 Interview one transcript
5 Interview two transcript

<button>Communicating Information – the main aim of this project was to produce material that communicated information about the new restaurant to the public. These files show how I have done this.

1 Document templates
2 Website designs
3 On-screen presentation of the menu and opening times
4 Pricing documentation

<button>Review – this section holds some of the most important documentation, developed from my research, testing and evaluation.

1 Original specification
2 Quality review record
3 Testimonials from the restaurant staff
4 Overall evaluation document
5 Proposals for future work

You will be given a new name for your home page and this must be stored in your **root directory** and clearly identified. Give it a name that will mean something to those who view it – normally a home page would be called index.htm, but on this occasion the page can be called something else, as it will not actually be a web-based page.

You should use something like your initials, candidate number and unit number, for example: DP_01234_Unit01.htm

Within the root directory you should set up a folder structure that enables easy navigation.

Possible structures

The specification contains details on the marks available for each piece of work. However, to help your teacher and anyone else who needs to assess your work, Edexcel have broken down the marks into six categories (Table 8.1).

Table 8.1

Category	Available marks
Plan and manage the project	0–5 marks
Select and capture information from a variety of sources	0–7 marks
Collate and analyse data to produce information	0–7 marks
Present and communicate information	0–9 marks
Present evidence in an e-portfolio	0–9 marks
Review the project	0–5 marks

You may be able to use variations on some of these six categories as your folder titles. Or you may wish to break down your e-portfolio into other sections, related to the evidence type each folder contains; for example:

- Images
- Spreadsheets
- Databases
- Paper publications
- On-screen publications

Each folder should contain an index page, with links to each file, making navigation very clear.

Each file must be clearly titled, and saved in a format that can be easily accessed through a browser.

Bear in mind that the marks mentioned in Table 8.1 for presenting the e-portfolio are awarded across *all* the material you submit – so you should not have a section, or folder, entitled 'presenting the e-portfolio'.

Intended audience

You should bear in mind at all times the *intended audience* – your teacher and the assessor and moderator. These last people may not know you or your work, so the only chance you have of letting them see your best and most relevant material is by very clear navigation around your e-portfolio.

A list of acceptable file formats will be issued by Edexcel, with the project brief. These are likely to be PDF for paper-based publications, **jpg** or **png** for images, html for on-screen publications and swf (Flash movie) for presentations, but this may be revised to take account of future developments.

PDF
portable document format

To enable you to work with these file types, you will need access to conversion applications. Your teacher will provide guidance on what is available to you in school. For home use you should have access to:

- A PDF generator, such as NovaPDF Printer
- A *PowerPoint* ® to *Flash* ® converter, such as *FlashPoint*
- Image conversion, available through most image manipulation software, such as Adobe *Photoshop* ®
- A compressing application might be useful as you work, but please note that Edexcel will not permit your e-portfolio to be compressed.

At the time of writing the total file size of the e-portfolio may be around 15 MB – that is not very big. Check with your tutor for exact details of the size allowed for your particular project. You must work out exactly what you need to include and then keep a close check on the size of the folder containing the e-portfolio.

You must present your e-portfolio content in a format appropriate for viewing at a resolution of 1024 × 768 pixels.

As with all websites, you must ensure that your materials follow the rules on accessibility. Where possible you should:

- Provide alternatives to auditory or visual content
- Avoid using colour for navigation
- Use simple, appropriate language
- Use tables
- Design your materials to work on any **platform**
- Provide clear navigation systems.

Before you submit your e-portfolio – test it! Carry out tests on a number of different machines, running different browsers.

> Remember: just because it works once, this does not mean it is reliable. Your qualification is resting on the reliability of your e-portfolio.

Clear identification

Each file must have a distinct title and a short explanation of its content.

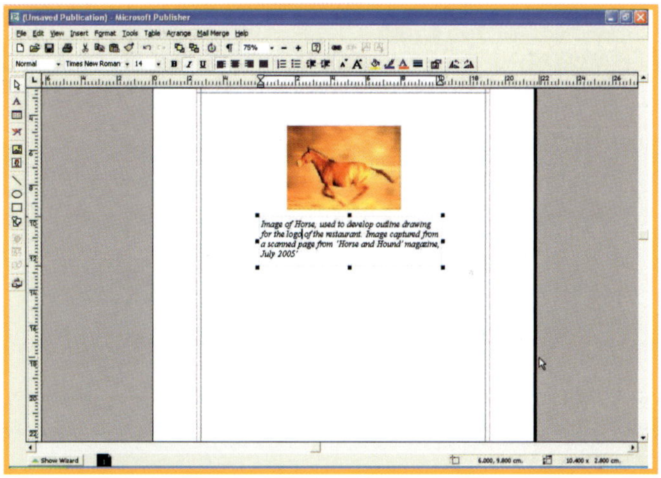

> Remember: you will know what everything is, but will someone who looks at your work for the first time?

It may be difficult to add comments to images. However, embedding the image in a desktop publishing (DTP) document and then adding your comment before converting the document to PDF may be a solution.

There may be similar problems with other file types. If you experience difficulties, it might be worth generating a short page of text as the main link, and then using a hyperlink from that to the file.

You will see from the sample database below that it is important to make the reader aware of any legal issues that you have had to take into account during your work. Any data that contains names and addresses comes under the Data Protection Act, so unless you have permission you must not pass these details to others.

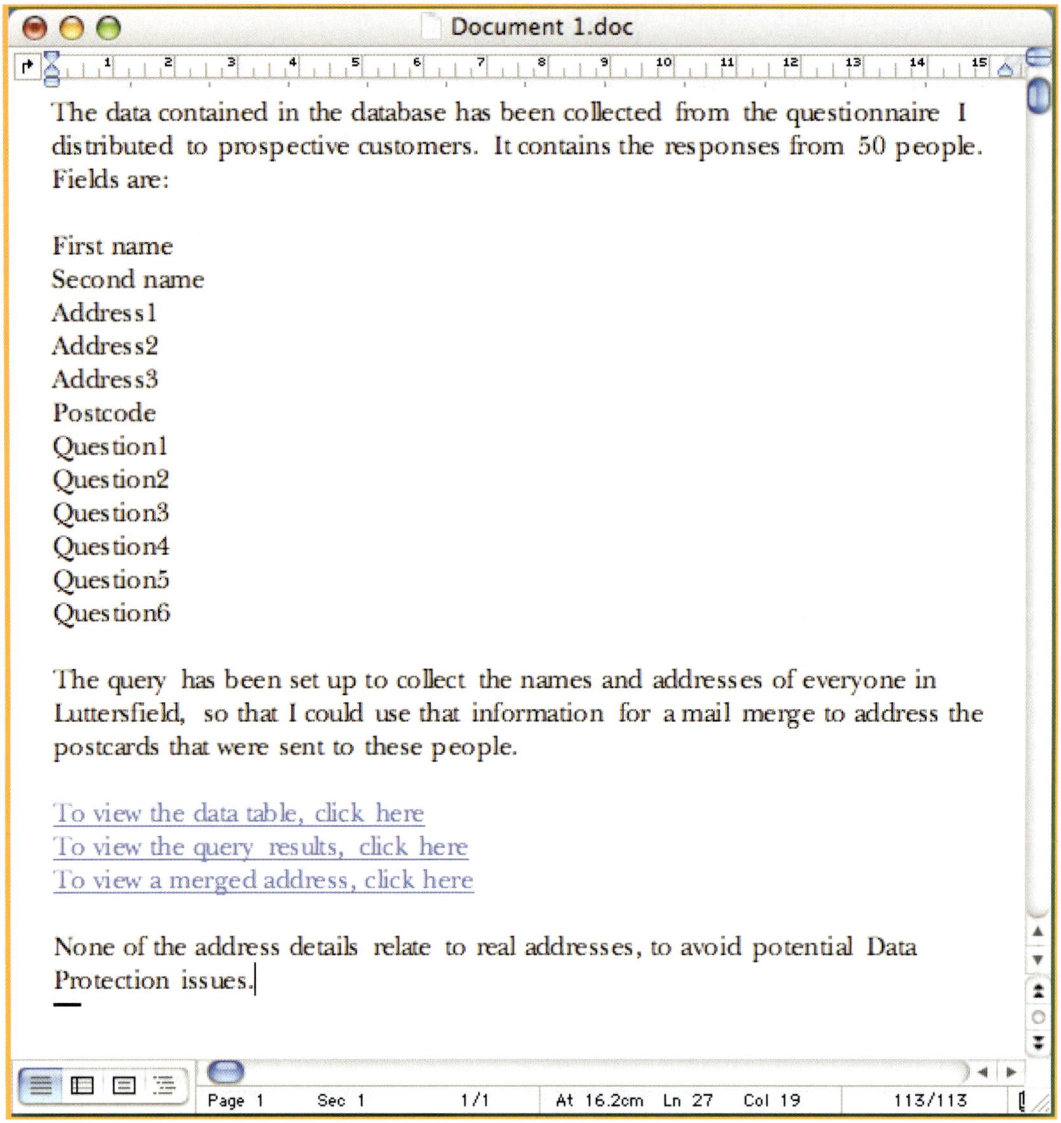

Document 1.doc

The data contained in the database has been collected from the questionnaire I distributed to prospective customers. It contains the responses from 50 people. Fields are:

First name
Second name
Address1
Address2
Address3
Postcode
Question1
Question2
Question3
Question4
Question5
Question6

The query has been set up to collect the names and addresses of everyone in Luttersfield, so that I could use that information for a mail merge to address the postcards that were sent to these people.

To view the data table, click here
To view the query results, click here
To view a merged address, click here

None of the address details relate to real addresses, to avoid potential Data Protection issues.

Sample database

There may also be copyright or other issues that you have had to deal with. If you have scanned an image, have you asked for permission to do so? If you have used some text from a book, have you recorded where it came from and acknowledged it in your work? Do you have permission to use photographs of people in your images folder?

Answers to these questions should be included in the commentary that accompanies each file.

Submission

By the time you submit your e-portfolio, you should have a complete package of files and folders, all clearly linked and accessed through a professional-looking home page.

- You will have tested it on a number of different machines, and asked others to test it for you.
- You will have incorporated the suggestions that the testers made, to improve your work.
- You will have checked every link and removed any that do not work.
- You will have checked that your e-portfolio contains everything that you need it to contain.
- You will have checked the total file size and made sure it is below the limit set by the awarding body – 15 MB.
- You will have checked that every file opens quickly and displays as expected.

Although your work may be submitted to the moderator electronically, using a secure Internet link, it is likely that you will be asked to submit a separate copy to your teacher, so that they can take it away with them for marking.

You should decide on the most appropriate method of submitting your e-portfolio. There are a number of options, as shown below.

Table 8.2

Format	Capacity	Advantages	Disadvantages
CD	700 MB	There is plenty of space Cheap (less than 10p per CD) Easy to print labels	Need a CD writer Lots of wasted capacity Can get scratched
USB memory stick	Up to 1 GB	Available in a variety of sizes Looks good Highly portable	Expensive (over £10 for 16 MB) Difficult to label
Flash memory	Up to 1 GB	Available in a variety of sizes Fast, easy to use	Expensive (over £10 for 16 MB) Need card reader

You should check with your teacher to make sure that the format you choose is acceptable. Although there are no marks for this aspect of the presentation of your e-portfolio, it does add a feeling of professionalism to your work. Don't be afraid to make it look good!

Homework

1. Experiment with some designs for the home page. Personalise it, but make sure it is smart and works well.
2. Ensure that you have access to the appropriate file conversion applications.
3. Check the accessibility rules at www.w3.org
4. Before you submit any work get one or more people to go through it. This is called testing and may highlight any problems. If possible, do this away from the classroom, perhaps at home, and evaluate your results.

CHAPTER 9

Project planning

What you will learn in this chapter

You will learn the skills needed to plan your project efficiently. You will learn how to allocate your time to each step of the project.

It will become clear very early on in your project whether or not your work has been planned. Project planning will help you to keep moving forward as you work. You will find you are not waiting for things or suddenly surprised by a problem that has loomed up! In industry, project planning is always done before a large project begins, because it will help people to decide what and whom they need, and when.

Each unit of the DiDA is assessed via a summative project in which students bring together the knowledge, skills and understanding they have acquired throughout the unit in one substantial piece of work. This is marked by the teacher and externally moderated. Students complete the project towards the end of the course.

The project is an important and sizeable piece of work, which must be done in school, college or wherever the learning is taking place. It is recommended that a minimum of 30 hours should be allowed for this project. Marks are awarded for project planning, selecting and capturing information, evaluation and the e-portfolio, in addition to the specific requirements of each of the four units.

It is easier to work through a plan of your project than to jump from one unplanned action to another. The planning, if done well, should speed you along, give you clear aims and objectives, help you to judge where you are in the whole project, and help maximise the marks you will be awarded.

When you have finished your project, review your work. You should evaluate the project outcomes and your own performance, including feedback from others and suggestions for improvement.

The specification

A specification is:

- The definition of your project
- A statement of the problem
- Not the solution.

To avoid months of activity working on the wrong project, the specification should be a *written* definition of what is required, by when; this must be *agreed* by all involved. There are no shortcuts to this; if you fail to spend the time initially, it will cost you far more later on.

A *written* specification has several benefits:

- It avoids misunderstandings.
- It highlights technical and practical details.
- It makes you think about the details.

Establishing controls

When the planning part is completed, the doing part begins. You need to establish at the start (within the plan) the means to monitor and to influence the project's progress. Milestones and timelines are key elements to the control of a project.

Milestones are a way for you to check that your project is still on track and that it has not taken too long to complete one particular task. They are, in effect, short-term goals, which are much easier to imagine completing than the overall long-term goal, which is the e-portfolio itself. If all the milestones that make up the e-portfolio are completed on time, then it follows that the e-portfolio itself will also be completed on time!

Because completing each milestone is less daunting than completing the whole e-portfolio, they help you to stay motivated and demonstrate that you are making progress towards completing the whole e-portfolio.

To construct some milestones, break your e-portfolio down into a series of sub-tasks; one sub-task, for instance, might be completing all your primary research through interviews and surveys. With your teacher or lecturer, work out how long you think each sub-task will take to complete and when it should be finished by. Remember that some sub-tasks could take place at the same time; equally, some sub-tasks might not be able to begin until a previous sub-task has ended.

Week 1
Planning

Week 2
Drawing up and distributing a questionnaire

Week 3
Writing up and interpreting results of questionnaire

Week 4
Preparing presentation

Week 5 (milestone)
The presentation

Week 6
Gathering and interpreting feedback from presentation and writing a report on how it went.

Timeline

A timeline is a linear plan that shows where you want to be each week, month or even day. It is a very visual guide that will help you decide if everything is running to time. You can highlight important achievements on the timeline and plan checks and feedback dates.

Once you have developed your timeline, **print it out** and stick it on a wall so that you can refer to it regularly.

Planning research

This usually takes longer than you think!

Research means finding out, to help you to be clear and confident in advance about what you are planning to do. Research needs to be done in an organised and systematic way. Often people research far more than they need to and spend much longer than they need to, which is why you need a clear plan!

As mentioned in Chapter 1 you can research using the Internet. If you use it well this is a fast and efficient method, but it is not the only method available to you. Asking the public through surveys, asking experts and interviewing people for their opinions are all methods used by businesses in industry. As you research you may need to discard everything but that which is directly of use to you. You do not have time to go off and investigate areas that may interest you but are irrelevant.

You need to plan for deadlines: your main deadline will be set for you, but it is a good idea for you to set yourself deadlines to get each stage of the project done – this will help you manage your work. You need to be absolutely clear about your objectives. Evaluation of your research methods may help you and others in the future, as you may be asked to research again.

Ask yourself:

- What went well and why?
- What would I do differently and what would I do again?
- Is the information correct and believable?

Common problems

There is a range of difficulties that may present themselves as you work through your project, but careful and accurate planning can enable you to avoid many of them. Some of the most common are listed below. Make sure you plan around them.

- Resources (i.e. computers, printers, digital cameras) are not always available.
- You have to complete unscheduled tasks.
- Often the initial estimate of the time required to complete tasks is wrong!

Task allocation

Make a list of what you need to do. You now have to allocate the tasks in a sensible order on your time plan – what is best to do first, second, and so on. Order these tasks so that they are performed in a sensible sequence.

Task allocation is not simply a case of sorting out the various tasks on your list to the time you have available. Think about what you can do now and what you need to prepare for, in order to work on other parts of your project.
In simple terms, consider what tasks you have to carry out and allocate sufficient time to the tasks to match that (give yourself a little extra time whenever possible).

If you need to learn something new, the task may be simplified by trying to work around it another way. If you lack confidence, break the tasks into smaller units, which can be completed easily.

Sometimes tasks can be grouped and allocated together. Some tasks which are seemingly independent may benefit from being done together since they use common ideas. For example, if you are using the library for references, you may also need to order a publication or ask for information. Always plan ahead: do not wait until you need something – make sure it is there ready for you when you need it.

Testing and quality

There is more detail on this in the next chapter, but here are some general ideas. No e-portfolio is complete without provision for testing. Each time you finish something, get it checked and ask for feedback. Try to get feedback from several people who you think can help you improve or offer constructive criticism.

When working out the schedule, therefore, you must allocate time for this part of each activity!

Fitness for purpose

As always, if you are enjoying what you are doing, you will probably be working and producing well. You are also more likely to realise when your work is at its best and stop there.

When thinking about how to produce your work try to use software that you are used to; do not spend too much time learning loads of new software if the software you know will do the job. Even in a simple programs such as Microsoft *Word* ®, you can produce websites, databases, posters, booklets and technical drawings. If you know how to use Adobe *Photoshop*® you can manipulate your images to a professional standard but you can do simple image manipulation in Microsoft *Word* ® too.

Planning for error

Things never quite work out how you think they will, so you must also plan for errors and unforeseen circumstances. For instance, what would happen if you planned every task within your e-portfolio so you knew exactly what you would be doing in every lesson throughout the year, and then you were ill for two weeks? Of course, you might not get ill at all, but if you did, your careful planning would be useless. By thinking about which elements of your project could go wrong at the planning stage, you will be more prepared if something unexpected does happen. You can make educated guesses as to where problems might lie – for instance, learning a brand new piece of software from scratch might not go as smoothly as you would hope, whereas if you are experienced at using email software then you could reasonably assume that this part of the project will not cause you many problems.

Finally

- Proofread your content on-screen. Check for spelling, but do not rely on your spellchecker as these will often put in a word that is similar to the one you misspelled but might be the wrong word. For example, 'fro' is a word: if you have misspelled 'for', it will leave it!
- Check everything works well and that what you intended to produce is actually functioning.
- Do not be too critical of your work before you have shown it to others. Testing usually includes showing your work to a group of people, not just yourself!
- Evaluate your work and try to be positive. Think about what went well and what you would change if you could do it again, if anything needs changing. Let others know what you enjoyed and which parts you are pleased about. Talk about your achievements.

At the end of any project, you should allocate time to review everything you have done. You should include information on both the work itself and the management of that work.

How to get good marks

- ✓ **Keep referring back to your plan and your objectives to see if you met them.**
- ✓ **Evaluate your objectives, whether you achieved them or not, and why.**
- ✓ **Get feedback from others and show what you think about what they have said and whether they were right.**
- ✓ **Consider the whole process of your project from beginning to end.**
- ✓ **Make some suggestions for improvements to your project and explain them.**

What will lose me marks?

- ✓ **If you do not refer to your plan.**
- ✓ **If your review of your objectives is merely a checklist, saying yes or no to each objective.**
- ✓ **If you do not mention feedback from others.**
- ✓ **If you just say what you did without explaining how or why.**
- ✓ **If you do not make valid suggestions for improvements.**

Homework

1 Try to research the meaning of your surname using different methods: the Internet and the library. You will need different strategies to use each method. If you are successful, write down a brief evaluation to see which method worked best for you and why.

2 Ask someone for feedback on your work, and ask them to tell you why they came to the decisions they made. Write down your findings and justify your decisions or modify accordingly.

3 Write out a timeline for your research. Check it with your tutor and agree a deadline and critical points in the planning.

4 Asking experts to help you could save time within your group. You may find, for example, that your parents have contacts that could help you. Make a list of professions, skills and hobbies that your contacts have, share these and build up a simple database as a group. Before you do this, you should make sure that everyone you plan to put on your database is happy to have their details stored in this way.

CHAPTER 10

Review and evaluation

What you will learn in this chapter

- You will learn how to check your work for relevance and accuracy.
- You will learn that reviewing (checking what you have done) can actually help you get things right.

Whenever you complete anything you should review it. We learn by our mistakes! We review things all the time; a football match is a good example, where the manager, players and fans think about what happened and suggest ways to improve in the future. The whole of this book is designed to help you get through this exciting new qualification. As we have put it together, we have constantly checked what we are doing to make sure we match the materials to the Edexcel specification. You need to do the same with your materials.

Much of your work will be in the form of a project. The previous chapter went through the sort of planning sequence you should follow. This chapter is concerned with how you can evaluate your work and use the results of the evaluation to better inform planning for future work.

Management of a project's stage

There are lots of different ways of working through a project, and as you get more competent you will start to take more control of the sequence yourself. However, whatever system you employ, there will always be stages. Each stage has a start, middle and end.

The start is characterised by the setting of the target – what you intend to achieve. For example:

- Produce a three-page essay on the Second World War
- Print a proof copy of a paper-based publication
- Add 20 records to the database

The middle is where it actually gets done, the activity takes place:

- Writing the essay
- Printing the proof copy
- Entering the 20 records

The end of a stage is where you can say, 'That is done, what's next?'

- You add the list of sources to the end of the essay
- The proof is fine and the final draft can go to print
- All 20 records are in and validated

Before you can start you must have a clear idea of what the stage will entail: a *specification*. This should be written in such a way that you could easily plan what you need to do and then use the specification to check against what you have done at the end of the stage.

- 1 The three-page essay should be approximately 600 words.

  2 You must include details of the role played by American media in the war.
- 1 The proof copy should be in draft monotone.

  2 There must be two copies, one for your records, one for the **proofreaders**.
- 1 The records are supplied in a set format, each record contains four data fields.

  2 Validation is automatic on two of the fields, the others must be checked manually.

  3 When each has been checked, add a tick in the checked field (field 5).

When you are happy with the specification, you should carry out the task. When you have fulfilled the needs of the specification, you should carry out a review. The review must use the specification as its basis:

- Does the essay have approximately 600 words over three sides?

  Have I included information on the role of the American media in the war?
- Is the proof copy draft monotone?

  Do I have two copies?

- Have I entered and checked the four fields per record?

  Has each record been ticked?

But usually it will also include some aspects of forward planning, developments that may be incorporated in the future to make the task easier, quicker or more efficient.

- Were any of the sources I used worth keeping for the future? Can I include them in my bookmarks folder?
- Can I get away with one draft copy for my records and getting the proofreading done on-screen?
- Could the data entry form be better designed? Is there another way the data can be entered?

For a comprehensive review and evaluation, the views of others would also be recorded:

- What mark did my teacher give the essay? What comments were made?
- Were the proofreaders happy with the copy?
- Was the data manager happy with the data entry?

Carrying out such a review at each stage of a project is an extremely useful activity. If the project is expected to run for a long period of time, such as a term in school, it is important that regular reviews are carried out, to ensure that everything is on track. One of the biggest problems traditional GCSE projects have revealed is that learners lose direction and end up doing something that is not what they set out to do.

Review and evaluation therefore, must, be built into the plan for the project. There may be particular stages that the project can be broken down into; these can then have end-of-stage evaluations. There may also be time-related checks; for example, 'by the end of week three, I will be able to review…'

This 'review plan' can be a very useful tool. In business, 'quality review' is an essential part of any project. In many organisations there are specialists employed to oversee quality and design quality assurance measures. One of these is the recording of reviews and evaluations in a quality log.

Other subjects already have such systems. Art students use a sketchbook where they record ideas, useful pictures, colour schemes or notes that they may use to influence their work in the future. Engineering students keep logbooks where they record processes, materials or tools that they may want to use in future work.

Quality log

To make your work stand out above that of other learners, you could develop a quality log of your own. In your file structure, make a new folder; title it 'quality log'. In the folder, start a **blog** – or document; call it 'DiDA Quality Log'. You should keep this file regularly updated with comments on what quality measures you have taken to ensure that your work is of the best possible standard.

This quality log can then be sent as part of your e-portfolio, to show the examiner how important reviews and evaluations have been in directing your work. At the end of a project, you can then pull together all the reviews and evaluations easily, as they will all be in one place – your quality log.

Blog
a 'web log' or online diary

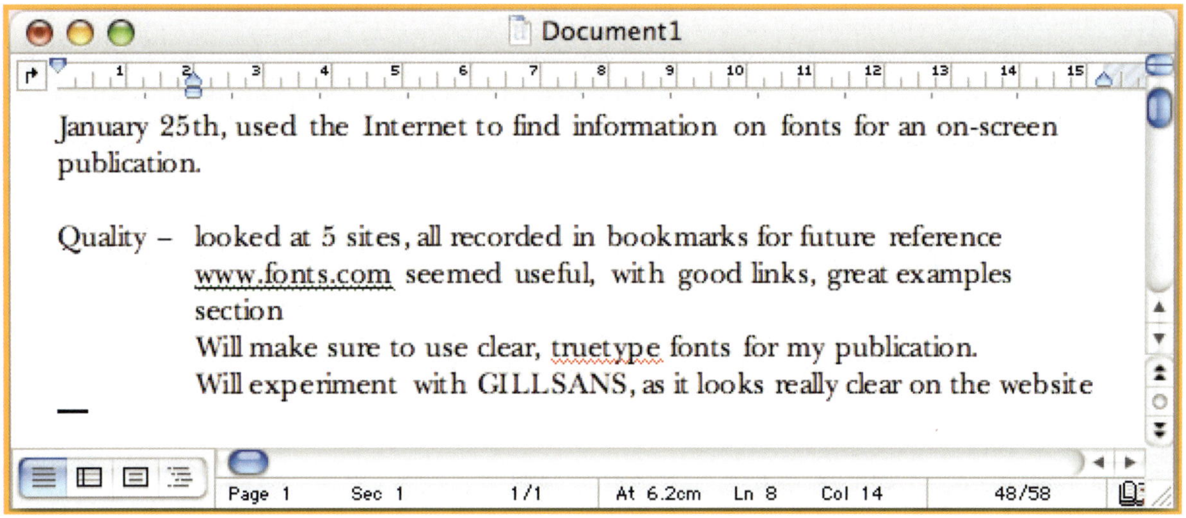

End of project review and evaluation

Although you will have had a regular quality check throughout your work, if you have set up your quality log, you will still need to produce a formal project evaluation. This is what will be marked by your teacher and sent to Edexcel.

In your project plan, you must set aside time to carry this out effectively. Ideally you will be contacting other people and getting them to pass comment on your work. If that is the case, they will need time to respond, so it is no good leaving your evaluation to the last lesson!

Throughout your project you will have been making comments about the effectiveness of your work. Now is when it all comes together to become a mark magnet! Your final evaluation must show that you have carried out a **thorough review**. Linking your evaluation to your quality log will show the marker that you have carried out regular and effective reviews throughout the project.

But you must also illustrate to the marker that you have tested and reviewed your final project outcome. This means that what you produce must go through some form of testing. All your materials will have been designed with a specific audience in mind and you must test your outcomes with the specified audience.

If you have been asked to produce an on-screen publication for preschool children, you must test it with preschool children. This will show the marker that you have ***real*** results from tests. Most learners will only test their work by themselves, or with others in their group. Make yours stand out – test it with real people.

If you have been asked to produce a design for a poster advertising a sports centre, there are three groups you should use in your evaluation:

- The staff at the sports centre – what do they think of the poster design. Does it compare well with other posters or publications that they presently use?
- The customers or clients of the sports centre – does it give them the information in a way that they find useful?
- A printer – is it possible to produce the poster in a professional manner?

When you are asking others about your work, you should try to gather the results in a useful format. You should consider using a questionnaire or some other *formal* recording system. Chapter 2 explained the need for closed questions; these are questions that try to force the respondent to say yes or no. Using closed questions in your evaluation can enable you to produce statistical results. For example:

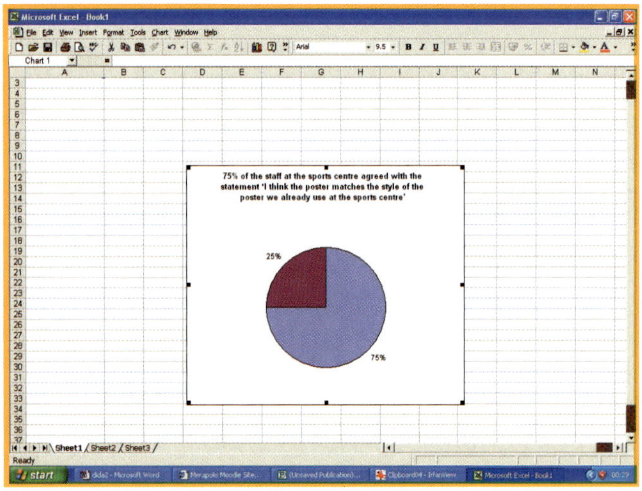

'75% of the staff at the sports centre agreed with the statement, "I think the poster matches the style of the advertisements we already use at the sports centre".'
Results that generate percentages can also be shown in graph or chart form.

Another technique is to ask people to score your work. Give them a range and ask them to award a figure:

'The sports centre customers awarded my poster 7 out of 10 for "How easy is it to read the information on the poster"?'

These sorts of results can be used to generate a bar chart, as each response can be recorded separately (see below).

A third data type you could seek from your reviewers is anecdotal comments. These are usually very difficult to quantify, so cannot be shown in a graph or chart, but can be very useful for showing how well your solution meets the specification: This sort of comment can be added as a quote: 'I think the work you have produced here is as good as anything my staff produce, well done', said the manager of the printing firm.

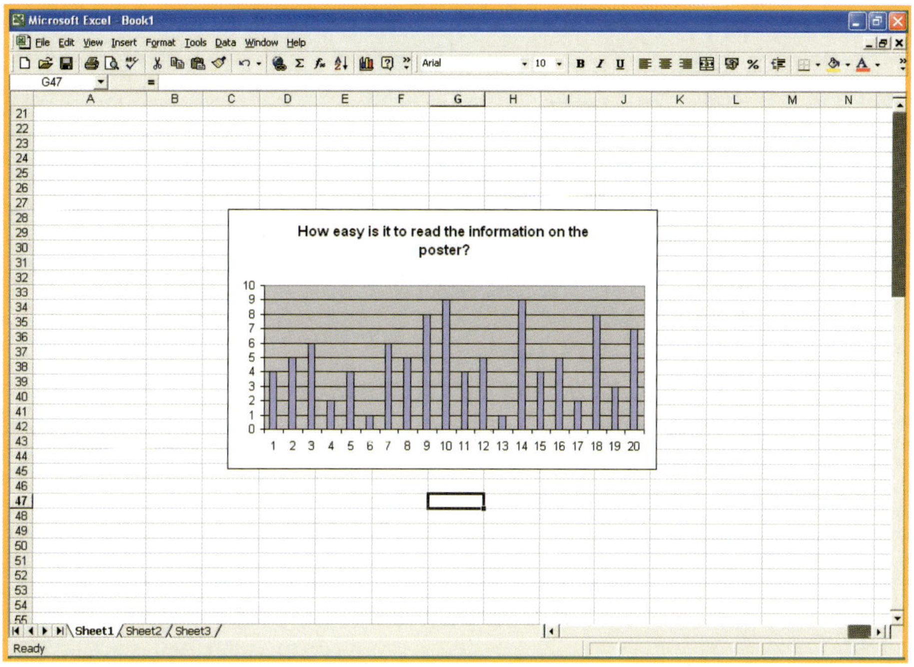

Harvesting information

When gathering data (in other words 'harvesting information') for your review, there are various methods you should employ and groups you could ask.

You may choose particular groups to harvest information from, other than the *real* users. These groups can be used to give general feedback, as well as offering specific details that relate to you and the DiDA course:

- Your teacher/lecturers
- Other members of your group
- Your peers (other people your age)

In business, a review may also involve a focus group, a small group that is representative of the normal clients or users. You could set up a focus group such as 'Sports Centre User Group'.

Whoever you choose to use, some methods may prove more successful than others. Questionnaires are very useful for asking lots of people the same thing. If you want to get some responses from a group of customers or staff, then a printed questionnaire is an efficient method. However, if you want information from one particular member of staff, such as the receptionist or manager, a questionnaire is probably not the best way.

When seeking the opinion of an individual you should try to interview them. This does not have to be done in person, but often speaking face to face is a great advantage. Sometimes it is difficult to get together, so you could try a telephone interview.

If you are unable to meet in person, you could try to meet online, using a *messenger* application or private chat room. Failing this, you could send the interviewee a set of questions and ask them to respond – but always include a deadline. One major problem with not carrying out the interview in person is that the interviewee may fail to respond in time for you to use their comments.

However you intend to carry out this type of information gathering, you must prepare. If possible, you should also brief the interviewee, so that they know what is expected of them. Before the 'meeting' you should carefully prepare your questions. Start off with some general questions, to relax both yourself and the interviewee, and then ask some more specific questions. Finish with an opportunity for the interviewee to give their general comments. Rather than taking notes as the interview is taking place, it is sometimes advisable to record the interview and transcribe it later.

Transcribe

Convert the recorded interview into text, by listening to the tape and typing the words into a suitable application

The whole thing should be scheduled to last no more than 15 minutes. Bear in mind that most TV interviews with politicians or others tend to last only 5 or 10 minutes. An intensive activity such as an interview can be very hard work. Try to restrict what you are trying to collect to the necessary and important bits.

When you have completed the interview, be sure to thank the interviewee for their time. Now you have the hard job of organising their responses. If possible, you should offer to send the interviewee the results from your information harvest. Sometimes this is difficult due to timing: the evaluation usually happens at the end of the project, close to the date when you will be submitting your work for assessment. But if there is time, you should send them a copy.

This is also something you should consider for your other results, but rather than sending them to the individuals, you could send them to the organisation for them to display:

- If you have been carrying out a survey of customers of a store, you could send the store the results, with an explanatory letter for them to display, to be seen by the customers.
- If you have asked the employees at a sports centre for their opinions concerning your poster design, you could send them a summary of the results, with a *thank-you* letter and a short explanation of how you will be using the results in your work.

Lessons learnt

Now that you have collected information from everyone and compiled the results into charts and graphs, what do you do with it?

Most evaluations are written at the end of a project. They tend to be very superficial – they usually say things like:

'I really enjoyed this project.
'I asked my mates and they said I had done a really good poster.'

Your teacher and the moderator will want to see more detail. If you have kept a record as you worked, and then carried out a survey or interview with the *real* users of your outcome, you should easily be able to put together a worthwhile and meaningful evaluation.

One part of an evaluation that is often poorly done, or just missed out in GCSE projects, is the 'lessons learnt' part. There are a number of reasons for carrying out an evaluation:

1. To formally state whether or not the original brief has been met.
2. To explain why particular aspects had to be the way they were, or why changes had to be made.
3. To celebrate the success of the project.
4. To detail changes that would need to be made to make the solution more successful.
5. To detail changes that would need to be made if the same project were to be tackled again.

The last two reasons are the ones that are often ignored. Make sure that your evaluations include them.

In industry, at the end of a project the manager will often commission a 'Lessons Learnt' document. This looks specifically at what went wrong and what went right, then puts forward a number of proposals that future project teams can follow. This is then used as the starting point of other projects.

Lessons learnt

* Quality of final print poor – colours are too dark and the images in the poster are not very clear.

  Suggestion – raise the contrast of the images before printing, check colour synch with printer by using a test sheet, test other printers

* Printing individual leaflets was costly and time-consuming.

  Suggestion – collect email addresses and email the leaflet to those with email, limit printed versions to minimum

* Data entry took hours!

  Suggestion – investigate optical mark reading (OMR) technology

Presenting your evaluation

In most cases your evaluation will be developed and presented as a word-processed document. This may then be used as the text of a web page or part of a DTP publication. However, there are other ways you may wish to try:

- An on-screen publication, presenting the information in a multimedia format
- A video – saved in an appropriate format to be viewed on the computer
- An interactive web page, where the user can select aspects of the evaluation that they feel are interesting.

Experiment with different approaches, and check with your teacher as to which method they think is most appropriate to the work you have been doing.

Homework

1 Develop a standard format for a quality log that enables you to record any review or evaluation opportunities as you work.
2 Keep your quality log up to date.
3 Produce a two-minute recorded evaluation of the successes and failures of your most recently marked piece of work for this unit. Try using Sound Recorder or similar software to produce the evaluation.

CHAPTER 11

Standard ways of working

What you will learn in this chapter

- You will learn how to work comfortably and in safety.
- You will learn how to manage your files efficiently.
- You will also touch on file types and how to use them.

Imagine the chaos if there were no rules about driving – if vehicles could drive at any speed, on either side of the road, there were no red lights, parking was wherever you stopped. It would be impossible to travel safely. Without sensible rules all systems become chaotic – it is the same in ICT.

I am sure you have worked on a document, saved it and closed the application, only to come along some time later and find that the file has 'disappeared'! Most people immediately blame the computer, or someone else, but invariably it is your own fault. If the file had been named sensibly and filed in a suitable place, it would have been found easily later. This chapter is all about working with ICT in an organised and logical way, following simple and sensible rules, so that not only you and your work improve, but everyone else is able to work efficiently and safely.

Before embarking on developing ICT-based materials, you must ensure that your machine is safe and free of virus infection. A virus checker and a **firewall** usually protect a school machine, but as you may be sharing material between your home and school computer, you must ensure that your home machine is equally safe. Just installing **antivirus software** is not good enough. You must make sure that it is up to date, and that it stays updated automatically. This is the same for all security software.

ICT is still a relatively new field. Although computer systems date back to the Second World War, until the last 20 years or so very few people worked with computers on a daily basis. This has meant that the ways of working in the industry are still evolving. New **legislation** and new **procedures** are developed, used and then amended. Then more new legislation and procedures need to be developed, and so on.

> Antivirus software can be downloaded relatively cheaply, but you may find that you can have a free version of your school's software. Ask your teacher.

The way that ICT has grown has also led to a different approach to the way legislation is drafted and put into practice. There has to be much more international agreement to make the world safer for users, as well as making international trade more efficient. ICT is often seen as a way of making things faster, more efficient and more reliable. This can only be the case if everyone works in the same way – a *standard way of working*.

There are also rules that you must follow. Some of these are legal requirements, such as the **Data Protection Act (DPA)**. Others are just sensible guidelines, such as being polite when using email.

Speed and reliability

One obvious advantage of using ICT to carry out certain tasks is the speed and reliability it brings. Modern processors can carry out billions of calculations per second, so they can work incredibly quickly.

Unfortunately, just increasing the speed of an operation does not make it more efficient. Imagine two vehicles, a family hatchback and a two-seater sports car. The sports car may be faster, but it is not so good at carrying four people and luggage, so would not be so efficient at taking a family on holiday.

To make ICT more efficient, speed is only one aspect to be considered. Things such as reliability (how often a new computer breaks down), whether it has connections to all the necessary **peripherals**, whether the software is easy to use, and so on, are also factors which affect efficiency.

The way you use ICT is also a great influence on the efficiency of the system. It helps to use the right application to carry out a task, such as a word processor for a letter rather than a spreadsheet, and to save your work in an organised way – for example, saving images in a folder labelled 'images'.

Health and safety

You should also consider the way in which you use the equipment and software, and the workspace that you operate in. (See also page xi.)

Workspace:

- Make sure that you have a safe environment in which to work, with no trailing wires or other obstructions.
- Position equipment away from direct sunlight.
- Position the screen so that your neck feels comfortable (a flat screen is usually the best type and should be anti-glare).
- Use well-designed furniture, to help with posture and comfort.
- The desk height should enable you to reach the keyboard and mouse easily.
- Use wrist rests on mouse mats and keyboards.
- Position equipment so you can use it without twisting.
- Have suitable lighting without glare.
- Take regular breaks from the computer, every 20 minutes or so.

If these rules are not followed, using computers can lead to:

- Backache
- Eye strain and headaches
- RSI (repetitive strain injury).

File management

Using a sensible method of filing is crucial. Everyone likes to work in their own way, but if people are working collaboratively, which is one of the advantages of using ICT, it is essential that everyone involved works together and uses a common approach to filing. All ICT users must make sure that data used is accurate, consistent and reliable, and that it is stored securely.

File names

The use of an appropriate file structure and naming conventions can help to ensure that data is stored in a way that will allow easy and efficient retrieval. All applications record the date and time of a document's use. If the user also gives it a suitable name it should make it easier to find at a later date.

The file type is also an important addition to a file name. Most operating systems have three-letter suffixes, or extensions, that denote the type of file. This is separated from the file name by a full stop, for example '.doc' for a word-processed document or '.xls' for a spreadsheet.

So, the application sets time and date and file type: all you have to do is supply a suitable name. Unfortunately, all software also generates default names, such as 'document1.doc' or 'sheet1.xls'. so you have to be a little more creative.

A letter to the bank manager could be entitled:

'Bank Manager Letter.doc'

Although most systems can accept spaces, it is probably best to avoid them. The same goes for capital letters. Use only lowercase, so the file name becomes:

'bankmanagerletter.doc'

As this can be a little confusing, the use of 'underscore' _ can take the place of the space, so the file name becomes:

'bankmanager_letter.doc'

As there may be more than one letter to be sent to the manager, or you may want to record replies, the use of a number can be advantageous, so the file name becomes:

'bankmanager_letter_01.doc

Older computer systems prefer fewer than eight letters before the suffix, and it does make titles easier to remember if they have fewer characters, so the file name becomes:

'bm_let01.doc'

As long as everyone knows the system, anybody who needs to have access to the first letter to the bank manager should be able to find it.

Backups

It is good practice to make backups of your data. Many systems automatically back up data overnight; your school's MIS (management information system) will probably back up at least once a week, so that if anything happens the bulk of the data is safe.

Disaster recovery is big business. Companies that lose data through fire or theft can go bankrupt. Imagine the difficulty an international supplier would have if they lost their sales records through someone pressing the wrong button! However, if backups and other systems are put in place, many disasters can be avoided.

Filing

When a system starts to get used there are only a few files, but in time this could well increase to many thousands – there are well over 500 files produced to write this book!

Remembering file names or the system used to generate them is one thing, but actually finding them is another. This is where the folder structure can be helpful.

Computer files can be stored in separate folders. This means that files that should be together can be grouped easily. For example:

- Images can be kept together in a folder named 'images'.
- Letters can be kept in a folder called 'correspondence'.

The structure containing the folders can also be carefully considered, making navigating through to a particular file a straightforward operation. This skill is an essential element of developing your e-portfolio, as you need to make it as easy as possible for the marker to find each of your pieces.

It is also important that the files are stored in an appropriate format. Although Adobe *Photoshop* is often used to manipulate graphical images, the format it uses to save images can only be read by Adobe applications. So if you were sharing an image it would be more appropriate, and sensible, to save it in a format that can be read by users who do not have access to *Photoshop*, such as jpeg. This may mean the image loses some of its functionality, but that may not be as important as others being able to see the image.

As mentioned in Chapter 8, PDFs (portable document files) are a generic file type that can be read by most machines. So saving a file in PDF format can mean that it is accessible by most people. However, unless they have specialist software, they will only be able to read the file, not amend it in any way.

Saving files

Many modern applications carry out an autosave every few minutes. This means that if anything happens, such as a power cut or the battery running out on a laptop, your work is not completely lost. However, this is not something to rely on. It is good practice to save your work regularly. I have saved this document twice in the last five minutes!

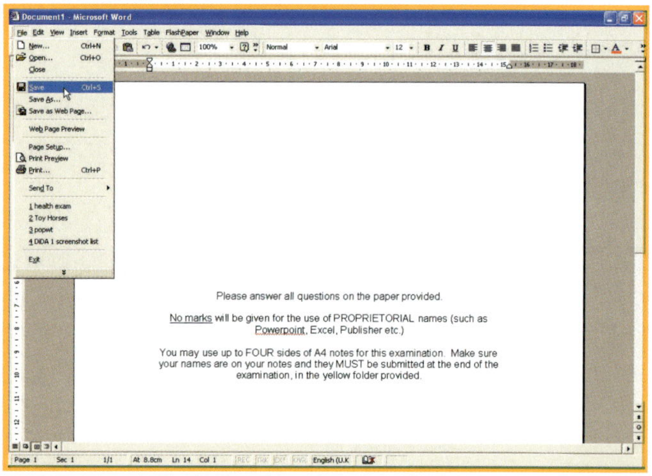

Sharing and security

If you work with others on a document, you may need to save different versions. If this is the case you can use the numbering system suggested above – 'bm_let01.doc', then 02, 03, 04, and so on.

It may also be advisable to set up a particular folder for shared material. If necessary the files and folder can also be protected by using passwords – check the help files of an application for guidance on how to do this for an individual file. You can use the operating system commands to share a folder over a network. Go to the Properties of the folder and select the section on Sharing. Depending on your operating system, you should be able to share a folder openly with any other user, or privately with particular users. There are also help sites on the Internet that can offer independent security advice.

If your colleagues are further afield, you can share materials through online storage facilities. Again, these can be secured with passwords.

Bear in mind that any files that contain personal data fall under the Data Protection Act and you must therefore ensure that they are kept securely, and that access is limited to individuals who have been given express permission.

Remember that any system is only as secure as the people using it want it to be. A password is a great way of stopping people accessing materials they are not supposed to, but if the password is not kept secure, the files will not be secure either! A similar thing is true with credit card personal identification numbers (PIN). They only work if the user does not give their number to anyone else or leave it for others to find.

If a folder has been set up to contain a number of specific files, it would also be sensible to include a listing of the files (a contents list) and instructions on what to do with them. It is good practice to do this using a 'readme' title for a text page. The page is usually stored in a '.txt' format, so that it can be opened in a range of applications.

The readme.txt file usually has a simple description of what can be found in the folder and who to contact if there is a difficulty (see below).

untitled

In this folder there are 16 files.
4 jpeg images: these will open in any graphics package.
8 text documents (excluding this readme): these are set to open in a text reader, they do not have any special formatting.
2 CSV files: these will open in a spreadsheet package.
1 short video clip: this should open in quicktime – you may have to download the latest version.
This readme file.
If you have a problem opening any of the files, email me: dave@my_email.co.uk

Using software effectively

If you can remember when you first started using ICT, you may remember that everything took a lot longer. Machines have not got that much better – you have. Over the time you have used computers, you will have learnt some **shortcuts**, such as using Ctrl C for copy and Ctrl V for paste, or using F1 for accessing the application *help files*.

Every software package has a vast array of helpful shortcuts. These are easily found when you look at a menu item. The menu bar itself has an underlined character in each title, the items on each menu also have one letter underlined. If you press 'Alt' and the letter in the title, the menu is expanded, and then to access the individual item you need to press 'Shift' and the underlined letter in the item. For example, to show the Task Pane in a Microsoft ® application, press Alt V followed by Shift K.

Some functions are common across many applications, such as copy and paste, but some only work in particular pieces of software.

Shortcuts can also be used to access common functions. If you look at your desktop, you will see a number of shortcut icons. When clicked, they carry out a particular function, such as opening a folder or starting an application. They are very useful tools for speeding up computer work.

You can create a shortcut by right-clicking on an item and choosing Create shortcut. The small file this creates can be cut and pasted to another location, but it will remember what it is a shortcut to! Adding shortcuts within a filing system can also be useful, as the shortcut can connect the user to files which are stored elsewhere on the system, without having to move or duplicate the files.

It also helps if you can choose the correct tool for a job – in manufacturing the skilled worker is the one who is best able to select and use the appropriate tool correctly. This is the same in ICT. Selecting the correct application and tools within an application will make you a much more efficient user of ICT.

Practice makes perfect.

Quality frameworks

A lot of good practice is common sense. Most of what has been mentioned above is sensible good practice. But to ensure that standards are raised it is important to work within a quality framework.

With modern **DTP** applications there is no excuse for poor spelling. Each software package has a **spellchecker**; most will also check grammar. Some systems have **thesaurus** and **dictionary** functions or even links to encyclopaedia entries. But even if the version you are working with does not have all this functionality, if you have access to the Internet you can get help with any aspect of your work by accessing websites that can perform checks for you, such as www.dictionary.com.

> Don't just copy chunks of data from encyclopaedia sites; the skill is in being able to adapt the material to your needs – copying is just plagiarism and easy to detect.

Checking

However, even with all the help tools working and checks being run constantly, you still need to check materials for yourself. **Proofreading** is essential for all documents, not just text documents. As mentioned in earlier chapters, data entered into a database or spreadsheet also needs to be checked to avoid data entry error.

If a document is to be printed you must also make sure that before printing you do a Print preview. This should be done every time a file is updated, prior to printing.

Earlier chapters also mentioned the need for getting other people to check your work, such as a sample audience. This can be a very useful tool, as you may not spot what other people find obvious – you may have spotted an error in this book that we never noticed.

You must also make sure that you recognise when others have helped you and record that in your work. This also goes for acknowledging any sources of information and authenticating your own work. You will be submitting an e-portfolio for assessment, which will have to be authenticated to prove that the work within it is yours. However, you must also point out where and how you have been helped.

By authenticating your work, you are stating that you have worked with standard ways of working, and in doing so have complied with all appropriate rules and regulations. You have acknowledged where you have used other people's work or ideas and sought and received help. You have also ensured that material that is confidential has been kept secure and only those with particular reason have had access to it.

As mentioned above, there are certain laws and guidelines that you also need to work within. The DPA is most often mentioned where ICT is concerned, but there are other laws that you need to be aware of (see Table 11.1).

Table 11.1

The Data Protection Act (DPA)	Controls how personal data is handled and distributed. Essential reading for anyone dealing with personal data.
The Health and Safety at Work Act	Covers health and safety in the workplace, to ensure that accidents are minimised. Just because you do not work there does not mean it is not a workplace! Other people do.
The Disability Discrimination Act (DDA)	Related to access for all, ensuring that people are not disadvantaged through physical disability or learning difficulty.
The Special Educational Needs Discrimination Act (SENDA)	Linked to the DDA, but more specifically for those with learning difficulties.
Copyright and Patents legislation	Covers all published materials and manufactured goods. If something is used for gain, it must be credited, and in most cases paid for.

Homework

1 Carry out an audit of your workspace. What can be done to improve it?

2 Make a help sheet on shortcuts that you use. This help sheet should be formatted for distribution over the Internet.

3 Use the Internet to investigate the legislation mentioned above. Produce a single-page report on each of them.

4 Design a page in a *Word®* document that explains to year 5 pupils what a folder is and how it could be used.

5 Do a six-point health and safety check of your school or college's ICT suite, then detail what could be improved, if anything.

CHAPTER 12

Artwork and image-editing software

What you will learn in this chapter

- You will learn about the image-editing software, scanning, artwork and names of tools common to this type of software.
- You will learn how to create exciting text and images.
- You will learn how to download free image-editing software that will cover all the needs for your course if you cannot use Adobe *Photoshop*.
- You will learn about cutting, copying and pasting images.
- You will learn about grouping and ungrouping objects.
- You will learn about the different types of effects you can use to alter images.

Artwork in the printing and graphics industry refers to any work that is finished and ready to be published or printed. It can be text on its own or text and images or images on their own. In an image-editing package you would probably put the final touches to an image before publishing.

Tip

It is easy to get carried away when you find out about all the exciting effects you can use with image-editing software. Spend a short-time trying them all out so that you are not tempted to go overboard when it comes to editing an image you will use in your project. Remember: don't use effects just because they are there!

Image editing

Software can change the colours, move selected parts of an image or add effects. In fact, the more powerful image-editing software packages, such as Adobe *Photoshop,* allow you to do just about anything to an image you can imagine! However, they are not just able to change images. Image-editing software can produce amazing typography (letters). You can even paint or draw and use the effects option to create brilliant designs. Most image-editing software would be used to prepare images for printing or to send to web pages as artwork and that is the main function of this kind of software. It is part of your creative toolbox.

Capturing images

You can capture images in many ways:

- Scanners
- Cameras
- Harvesting from the Internet
- Buying images from image libraries (expensive)
- Clip art libraries.

There are two types of scanner you are likely to come across. Most people have a **flatbed scanner**.

With this machine you lay your book or image on top, face down, and the machine scans across the image. The information is then processed by the scanning software on your computer. This type of scanner is ideal for thick materials or larger images.

The other kind is usually incorporated into a printer and the material to be scanned is fed through the machine in the same way as you would do when printing. These machines are good because you do not have to buy a separate scanner, so they take up less space on your desk, but of course you can only pass through images that are on thin paper or card and that are no larger than the paper size the printer can take, usually A4.

Most scanning software allows you to do a prescan. A prescan scans the whole bed, then allows you to make decisions on size or **cropping**. The resolution can also be set;
300 dpi (dots per inch) is usually fine. For Internet images 100 dpi is high enough, as monitor screens usually run at about 72 dpi. The higher the resolution, the more space the file will take up in your computer's memory.

You can set your scanner to work directly from Microsoft *Word* ® and many other applications, or directly into your image-editing software.

Most scanning software will allow you to do some image editing before you scan. Size, **contrast** and cropping are all usual options. Some scanning software has a lot more functionality and it usually comes free with the scanner.

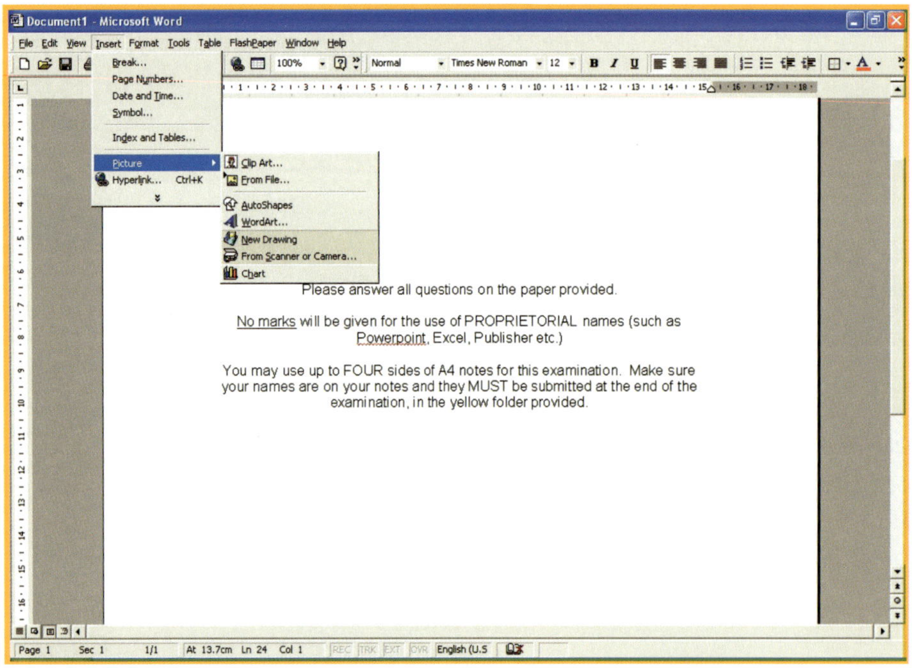

Image editors

You can tweak photographs taken with a digital camera, scan in images and create original images using a good imaging tool. Low-end packages let you do basic visual manipulations, such as adjusting brightness or cropping the picture. In Microsoft *Word* ®, for instance, you can scan an image, then adjust it using the image control tools on the highlighted work. You can also crop poorly composed shots using the cropping tool, by dragging it over your work until it is the size you require.

In the industry standard software packages, such as Adobe *Photoshop,* you can do just about anything! Image-editing packages are often based on what used to happen before computers were involved. All image setting was done either in a darkroom by skilled photographers using light and chemicals, or by skilled **retouching** artists who painted and **airbrush**ed details or highlights. These jobs can all be done in most image-editing software today. Packages like Adobe *Photoshop* provide tools to radically change an image and save it in many different ways.

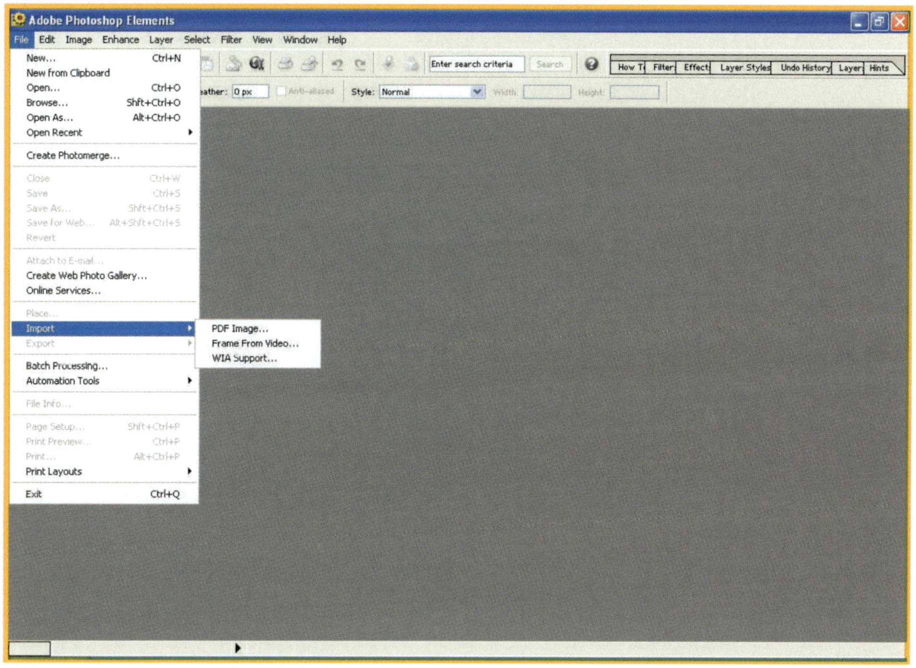

Adobe is the software publisher best known for graphics. Their imaging software includes Adobe *Photoshop*, Adobe *ImageReady*, Adobe *Illustrator* ® and Adobe *Photoshop Elements*.

Macromedia also produces popular software – Macromedia *Fireworks* ® has replaced Adobe *Photoshop* in some cases as a standard for producing web-based visuals. There are many others, such as *Corel Draw* ® and *AppleWorks* ®.

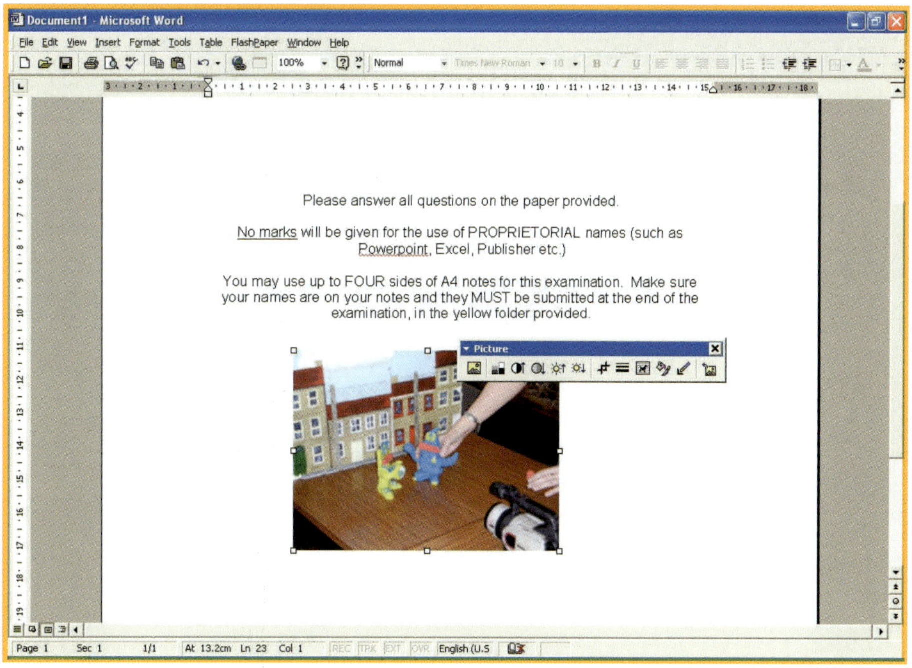

Once your image is stored on the computer you can start to manipulate it. A scanner can be used to get the image onto the computer, but there are other ways. Cameras can be connected by leads, usually to a **USB port**, but many cameras use **memory cards** and these can be inserted into a card reader which will read the digitally stored information and transfer your photos to the computer.

But what do you do if you want an image of, say, the Statue of Liberty in New York? Flying there could take time and would be expensive! What you can do is look for clip art libraries. Clip art libraries do not only have cartoon images. If you do an Internet search you may also find thousands of copyright-free images that you can download. The advantage of clip art is that the images are done for you so you do not have to generate them yourself. Clip CD-ROMs can also be purchased or found free on magazine covers.

Adobe *Photoshop*

Adobe *Photoshop* ® software is one of the most popular desktop image-editing and graphic manipulation packages. You can use it to make original artwork, scan in images or transform images. Tools and **filters** can help you to adjust brightness, contrast and colour, along with retouching and reinventing pictures. The images can then be saved in many file formats.

Although this skills section describes *Photoshop*, most of the tools are common across a wide range of image-editing and graphics software. Cropping, contrast adjustment and brush-sizing shortcuts nearly all work in all types of graphics/image-editing software.

The tools

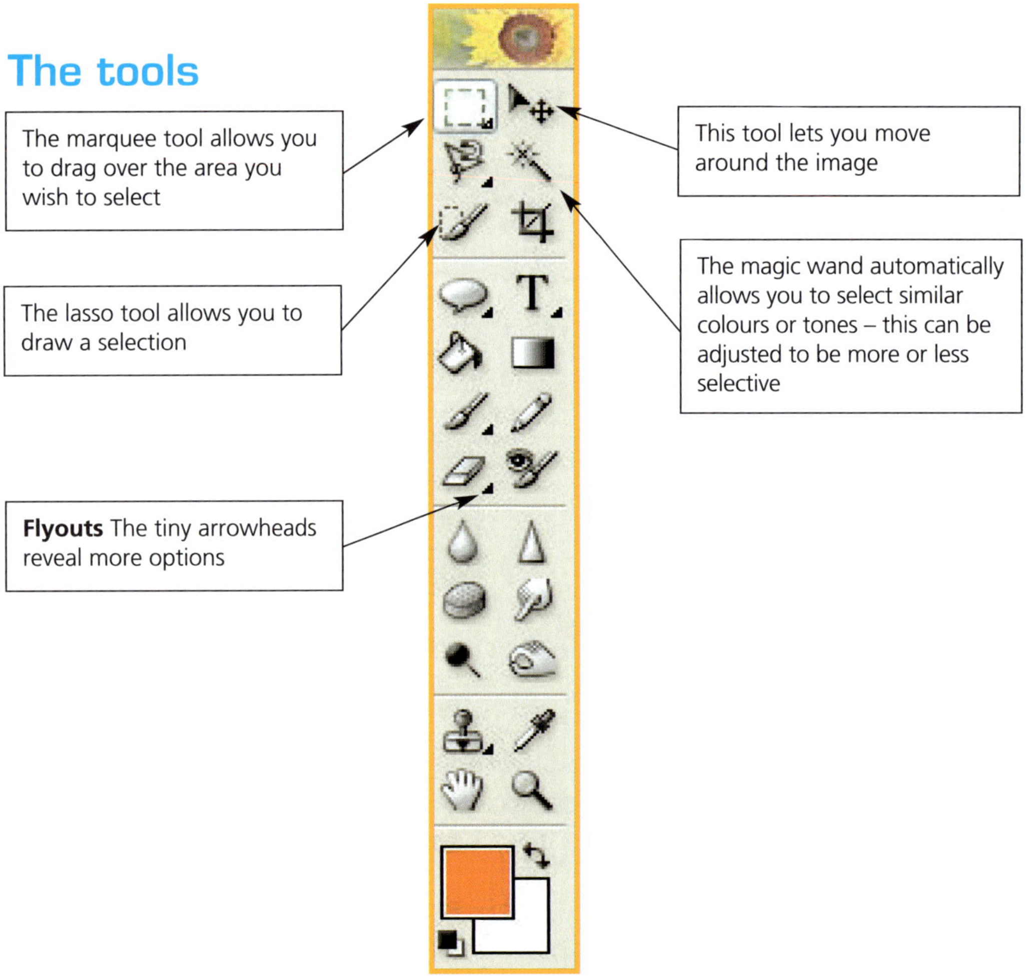

Although the mouse has made graphics applications a possibility, as the pointer can be moved around the screen like a pencil or brush, most *Photoshop* commands can be carried out via the keyboard.

Mac users: substitute the Command key for the Control key.

To enable you to use the application efficiently, it will help to learn some common keystrokes.

Ctrl+A	Select all
Ctrl+C	Copy
Ctrl+V	Paste
Ctrl+S	Save
Ctrl+D	Deselect
Ctrl+Z	Undo
Ctrl+U	Adjust hue/saturation
Ctrl+X	Cut (useful for layers)

The tools palette in *Photoshop* and similar programs can be huge. Because of this, many of the tools and palettes are hidden until they are needed. In *Photoshop* these toolbars have tiny arrowheads that reveal further tools when clicked on. This is a common feature, which saves the screen from becoming cluttered up with dialogue boxes.

In this type of software, images can use up huge amounts of memory, which can cause your computer to crash or work really slowly. For this reason *Photoshop* reveals the memory size of the image you are working on in the bottom left-hand corner of the frame.

Zooming in and out of your images using the magnifying tool or the navigator tool does not alter the physical size of the image (the size it will print out at). To change the size of the image, either to save memory or for sizing correctly on the page, you can use the Transform option, which is under the Edit option. This allows you to scale the image manually. Another method is to resize using the Image resize option.

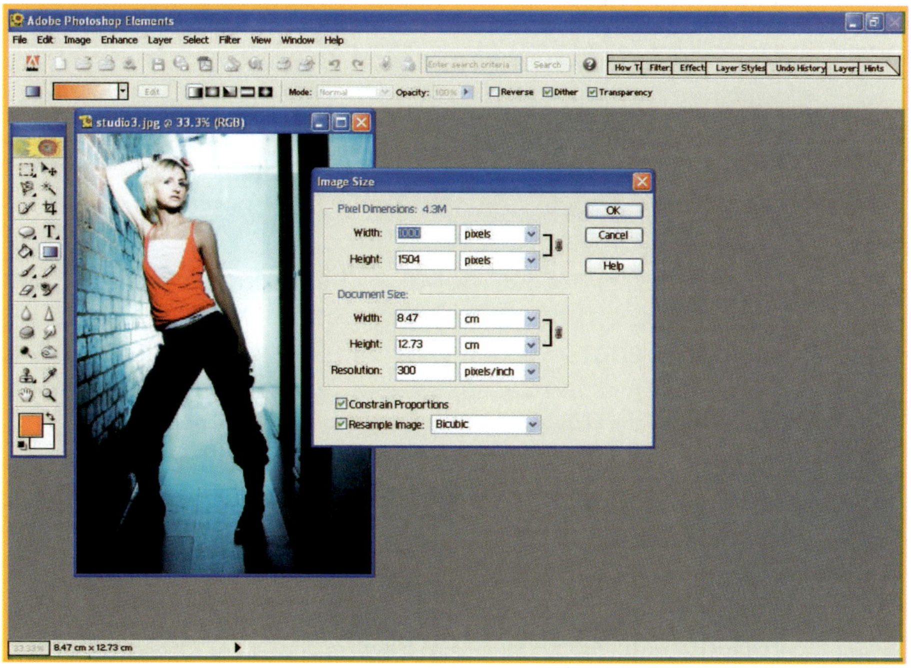

This process allows you to scale down the image to precisely the size you require. This is usually done in centimetres, but you can also use percentages.

If you do not have the constraint proportions box ticked when you do the resizing, the image will become distorted or stretched.

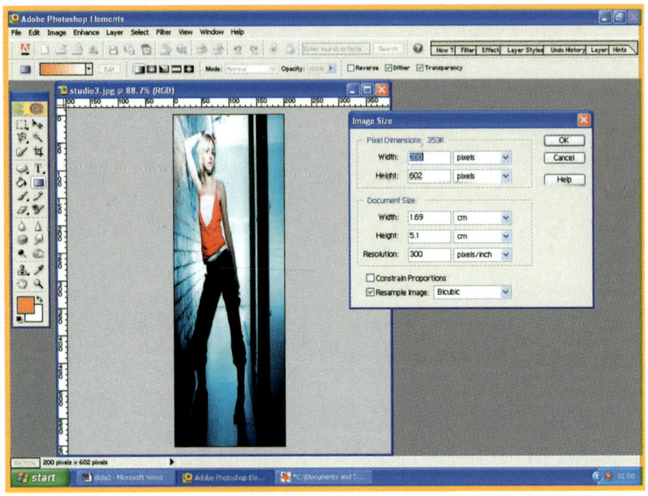

If you were producing artwork professionally you would probably use *Photoshop* for changing your images. *Photoshop* and similar image manipulation packages, such as *Illustrator* or *Corel Draw*, also allow you to work on typography, images and colour. Desktop publishing packages, such as Microsoft *Publisher* ®, Adobe *PageMaker* ®, or *Quark XPress* ®, allow you to create the pages for a publication by adding files from the image packages mentioned above. For web authoring and design you may use all or some of the above, plus specific web design software. Most of the software I have mentioned is used by design and printing businesses throughout the world – they are industry standard packages. There are often different versions of the same software package. *Photoshop*, for instance, comes in two versions – *Photoshop Elements* is a version of *Photoshop* that will more than cover the needs of most home and educational users, but is a fraction of the cost of the full version. It has fewer features, but it will do all you need for DiDA.

Most image-editing software is based on processes that years ago were done in a darkroom with wet papers and chemicals. Even the finishing processes, such as airbrushing and **spotting out**, retouching and adding effects, can now be done on screen instead of in a darkroom. For instance, adding blur effects can be done by going to Effects and choosing one of the many blur options; adjusting the colour can be done in image adjustments using on-screen sliders.

Photoshop is not just about editing images, you can produce some really amazing type effects, using the Layers option to create letters that are embossed or have coloured edges, or text that takes up different shapes. Text effects created in *Photoshop* or similar image-editing software can look stunning and are really easy to do. Possibly the easiest way to have fun with text is to apply effects. These can be controlled with sliders and can make relatively dull-looking headlines really interesting. The text effect can be used successfully on text for the screen, as part of a website or on printed material.

Text can also have shadows or drop shadows applied, once again from the Layer option. This process really looks especially good on titles and headlines. Do not forget,

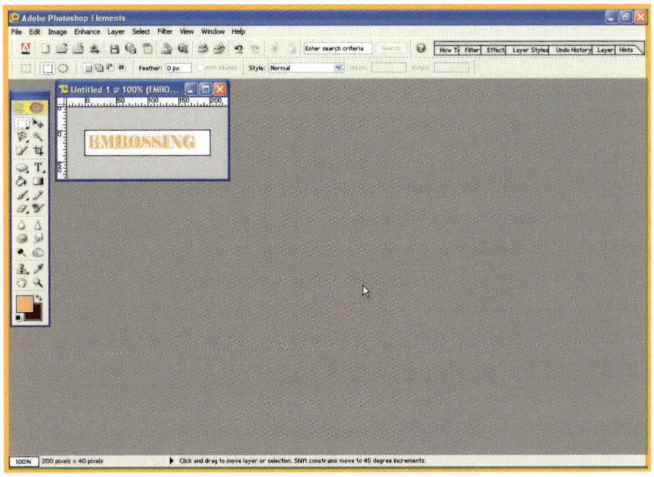

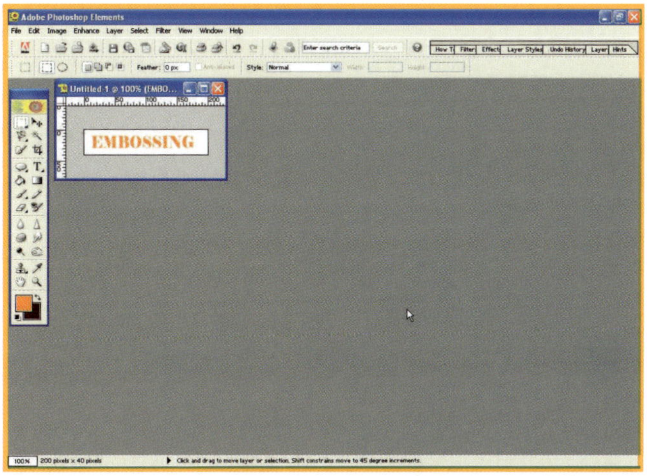

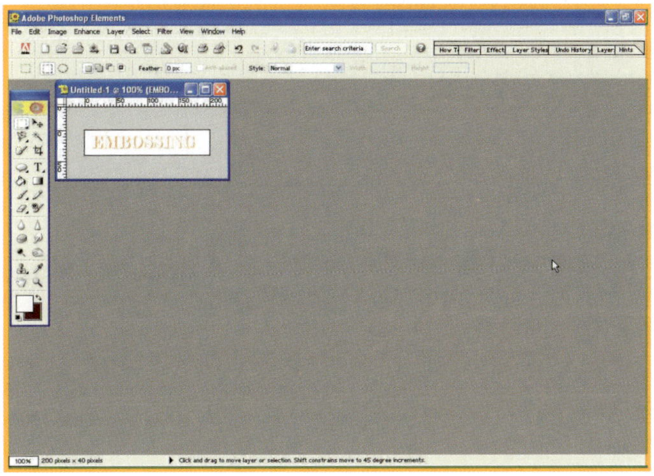

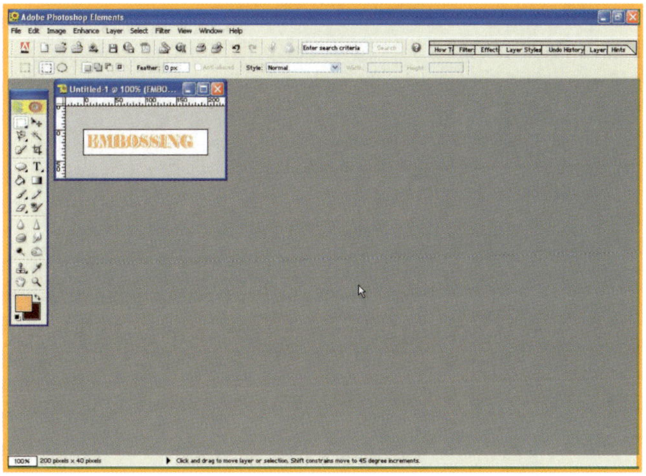

of course, that you can apply all the power of an image-editing package to any of your hand-drawn artwork or images by scanning the work directly into the software. In fact, if you have access to a scanner, you can apply the power of the software to objects such as leaves, twigs, shells, peel, bark, stones, flowers, and so on. All these scan surprisingly well! You must ask whoever owns the scanner before scanning such items in, however. You must also be careful with the glass base of the scanner and refrain from looking at the light as it passes over the scanning bed.

Image manipulation software is used by graphic designers, web designers, fashion designers and artists. Many people are surprised by the statement that artists use *Photoshop,* but interestingly the package has most of the tools an art studio would have: brushes of any size or shape, airbrushes and a huge range of colours and textures.

Image manipulation software can produce textured backgrounds to artwork such as canvas, weaves, and so on. To add textures to an image or part of an image you can go to the Effects option and search out filters such as Noise, which gives a dotted texture to grainy clouding textures.

Brushes can also be adjusted to suit your needs. The usual options allow you to alter the shaping of the tips as well as the width and edge effects.

To create hard or soft edges

Soft edges are usually more useful as they can blend each brushstroke and look more realistic. The selection tools can be used in the same way as brushes, with hard edges or with soft edges. When you click on any selection tool, an option appears on the top of your screen called Feathering which allows you to have soft edges. What you have to do is select the feathering value before you select anything on the image you are working on. Once you put a value in the feathering box you can select the image. The feathering option allows for a fade to transparency. The need for a soft edge on selection tools becomes more obvious when you cut out an image and paste it onto a background; the soft edge makes the image look naturally in place. Feathering can also create a great effect on an image placed into text. The effects of feathering edges can be seen in many magazines and newspapers and is a very popular tool with graphic designer.

One of the most useful selection tools, which once again can be used with or without feathering, is the magic wand.

This tool, when selected, has a tolerance which means that instead of drawing around a part of your image, it seeks out similar colours or tones to the pixel you have clicked with it. For instance, if you had a very blue sky and needed to change the brightness or remove the blue and put in grey, the magic wand will seek out all the blue and allow you to delete or work on the blue areas. The tolerance level helps it to decide how much blue or how little you wish to remove. A low tolerance will mean it seeks very similar colours to the spot you first click into; a high tolerance means it is less fussy and will seek general blues (or whatever colour you click on). The magic wand is available in many graphics packages and is designed to help speed up work by automatically seeking the colours or tones you wish to work with.

Selection tools always show you what you have selected by putting 'marching ants' around the selected area. Marching ants are the little dots that move around the selected area

----

Zooming

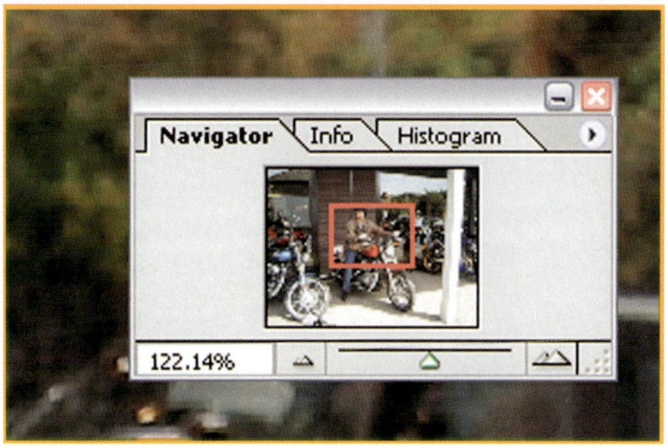

Eye strain is a very important issue with any screen-based software, so rather than use the magnifying glass, try to use the navigator tool, which you should set up as soon as the software is loaded. Navigation tools allow you to zoom in and out quickly and to move rapidly around a zoomed image. There is little point in straining your eyes looking at a tiny image when you can easily zoom in and out with this tool.

Layers

Most graphics software has a layers option and for DiDA it is important that you understand how these work. Layers are a bit like glass sheets that separate different images. Each time you add a layer you create a separate glass sheet to work on. In the same way that you cannot paint through glass, the image you are working on cannot affect the image below.

Try this

1. Load up the Layers dialogue box.
2. On the background layer paint some brushstrokes using a bold brush.
3. Put in a new layer by clicking on the New layer option.
4. Brush over this layer covering the layer, with paint. Now get a rubber from the toolbox and rub out to reveal the layer below.

In *Photoshop* you can add many layers and link some layers using the chain icon, this will link some changes, such as transformation and position on the layer.

The best way to learn how to use layers is to cut and paste a few images onto a set of layers and either rub away part of each image or use the Transparency option in the Layers dialogue box to fade one layer into the other.

Transform

The Transform option allows you to scale, flip, rotate, distort and create perspective to your image or text. In *Photoshop* you are given handles to pull or stretch your image. Handles normally appear on any object that can be resized. This includes image and text boxes in Microsoft *Word* ® and most other software.

Tip

To view option boxes, colour palettes, layers, and so on, you usually go to window and click on the ones you need – unless you have a huge screen it is best to **only** view the boxes you need.

Grouping and ungrouping objects

Grouping is common practice for computer-based designers. Grouping allows you to join several objects together to form one object to move around and work on. Grouping can be done in just about every graphics program and most Microsoft ® packages. To group objects you click on the first and hold down the Shift key, which allows you to click and add further objects. Once you have done this, go to the Group command. In Microsoft *Word* ® the Group command can be found in the Drawing toolbar under, Draw > Order. You can also drag a **marquee** (drag the mouse with the left button held down over a group of objects – 'objects' could mean drawn shapes, a group of pictures or a group of parts you wish to make into a whole).

Once objects are grouped they can have actions applied to them as though they were one object; for instance, they can be coloured, sized or flipped all at once instead of one at a time.

You can ungroup objects simply by clicking on Ungroup in the same menu in which you found Group.

Cut, copy and paste

These commands are the basis to most computer work concerned with writing or graphic design. They are based on old-fashioned graphics processes where you literally cut things out of paper and pasted them elsewhere on your design by hand. This was common to making magazines and newspapers. These terms have now moved to the computer and mean basically the same thing.

How to cut something

Simply highlight it if it is text or select it if it is an object or image.

Go to the Edit menu and click Cut, the object disappears.
When you decide where you want the cut object to go, put your cursor there.

Select the Edit menu and click on Paste and it will reappear.

You can paste as many times as you like and that object will stay there until you cut another object.

How to copy images and text

Copying uses exactly the same process except you select Copy from the Edit menu and paste in the same way, Edit and Paste! The difference between cutting and copying is that rather than 'cutting' the material out, you are copying it, so the original text or image stays where it was.

In virtually all software the following shortcuts apply:

Press Control and X **on selected items to** Cut
Press Control and C **to** Copy **an item**
Press Control and V **to** Paste

Flipping and reversing using Microsoft Office® software

To flip or reverse a shape or object, you first need to select it – you do this by clicking on it. The computer will now know that you wish to work on that item. Go to the Draw menu and select Flip. Then choose Vertical (if you want to flip the object up or down) or Horizontal (if you want to flip the object from side to side). In most graphics software, such as Adobe *Photoshop*, you can find the flip commands under the Transform menu, rather than the Draw menu.

To rotate your page and change it from portrait (the page is taller than it is wide) to landscape (the page is wider than it is tall) and back, go to File>Page Setup and select the Paper tab. This will allow you to switch between portrait and landscape without altering the actual dimensions of the page. Using a landscape page is useful for printing off drawings or plans that are too wide to be printed as portrait pages.

Homework

1 This is the best homework ever! Go to Picasa. What is Picasa? It is free image-editing software, so no excuses any more. Picasa software allows you to view, edit and organise your images. To find out more, go to http://picasa.google.com/index.html where you can download the software for free.

CHAPTER 13 Database software

What you will learn in this chapter

This chapter will help you to develop simple databases. The methods shown are similar across a range of database software; some of the jargon and menus will be similar in similar packages. Most people, however, will have Microsoft *Access*®. You will learn how to plan and test your database.

In Chapter 3 the idea of storing data in an electronic format was discussed. This chapter looks into it a bit further and will guide you through developing a database suitable for use as evidence in your e-portfolio. Your SPB will give you specific details about the database you will be expected to create.

Databases are basically made up from tables, the simplest form being called a **flat file database**. When databases started to be developed using ICT, this format was adopted as it seemed the most straightforward:

- Data is stored in a single table
- Each row in the table is a record
- Each column in the table is a field.

Table 13.1

	Field a	Field b	Field c	Field n
Record 1				
Record 2				
Record 3				
Record x				

The data can be searched or interrogated easily and quickly, as it is a simple arrangement.

However, as databases became more complex, holding greater amounts of data, it became necessary to rethink the way data was being stored. Part of the reason for this was the size of the file; a table holding thousands or millions of records is a pretty big table!

Unfortunately for computers, every cell in the table took up space, whether it held data or not. This added to the size of the file and the speed at which data could be searched. As with all things to do with ICT, it was decided that the files needed to be smaller and search speeds had to be faster – the only way to do this, at the time, was to radically alter the way databases were constructed. This led to the development of multi-table databases, or **relational databases**.

A relational database uses a number of linked tables, each one holding a specific data set. In this format large amounts of data can be stored in a smaller file, and each table can be searched quickly; therefore the two criteria of size and speed are met.

DiDA requires that all learners use skills and techniques appropriate to the task, and in the case of databases, it is unlikely that anyone studying at GCSE level will need to handle enough data to warrant the use of a relational database.

The two criteria of file size and speed are irrelevant when working with small data sets. As you will only need to store and manipulate a few hundred data entries, the file size is going to be tiny and access speeds will be instantaneous. As most computers now work at such high speeds and can store incredible amounts of data, the role of relational databases is less crucial.

You need to be able to design and use a flat file database. So… what are you going to do?

TASK: Use information from a number of sources to develop a database that can be interrogated to produce a quotation for a customer concerning the purchase of a laptop computer.

The following exercise will take you through all the relevant stages in working with a flat file database. At each stage you are told exactly what to do and how to do it. If you have any problems, retrace your steps and start again. If you come across something you do not understand, ask your teacher, or access the help files of the application you are using.

Creating a database

Before you can start to design or create a database on the computer you must work out what the fields are going to be and what they are likely to contain. To be able to do this you will need to do some research. The task asks you to develop a database to store details about computer equipment. Table 3.1 gives a possible set of fields, but it is not the only possible solution.

Table 13.2

Field name	Date type	Size of field
Manufacturer	text	30
Price	currency	6
Delivery cost	currency	5
Processor type	text	15
Processor speed	number	3
HDD size	number	3
RAM	number	4
Screen size	mixed	10
Bluetooth	yes/no	
Graphic memory	number	4
DVD writer	yes/no	

Table 13.2 *Continued*

Field name	Date type	Size of field
USB2	number	1
USB1	number	1
Firewire	yes/no	
Infrared	yes/no	
Operating system	lookup	
Bundled software	text	100

When you have decided on field names and data types, you will need to get cracking with your database application.

For this exercise the details are for the Microsoft *Access 2002* ® database program, although most database and spreadsheet applications are similar.

Using Microsoft Access®

Open the database application. You may be welcomed with a wizard asking what you would like to do – close that, we are going to start at the beginning.

We will start with a 'blank database', so choose that from the New File menu.

Because of the nature of databases, you must save a database before you start to work with it. This sets up an area on the computer that the application will access as you work. Give the database a filename – not db1! – and make a note of where it is saved.

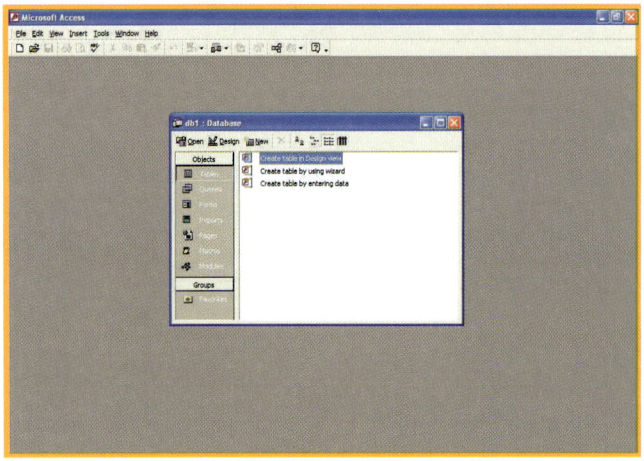

The first thing to do is set up the table that will be the root data set for all future work. There are different ways of creating a table; the easiest way is to work in Design view. In Design view you can enter the field names and data type directly into the database structure. Using the wizard can complicate matters: entering data is fine, but you have to go back later and rename fields and that is something that can prove difficult.

You now need to enter your field names and data types and then save the structure.

Before you start entering any data, check it by looking at the table you have just developed in Datasheet view.

If you have used a similar set of fields as those suggested in Table 13.1, you will have different data types, including yes/no check boxes. These are straightforward, but if you have used a **lookup** table you will have to build the lookup – you will need to enter the possible selections, so that when it comes to adding the data, you will just click on the one choice that is most appropriate. In earlier chapters it has been mentioned that data entry is the most likely place for errors to happen. A 'lookup' can make it easier to get the entry correct every time.

If it looks all right, you can start to enter data. The application will save all changes to the table as you work, as it has already set up a space and now a table to save into.

How to create a lookup

1. Move to an area of the data sheet that you will not be using for the main data.
2. Add a column heading – 'pick lists'.
3. Move down to a blank row and enter 'yes'; in the cell immediately below, enter 'no'.
4. Click in the cell where you want the option list to appear.
5. Go to Data on the menu bar (or press Alt D) and then click Validation (or press Shift I).
6. In the 'Allow' box, choose 'List'.
7. The option to enter a 'source' will appear – you need to add the cell references for the 'yes' and 'no' you have just entered. The easiest way is to click in the 'yes' cell and drag to the 'no' cell. To do this, minimise the Data Validation dialogue box by clicking on the graphic in the 'Source' box, then click in the appropriate cells.
8. You can add an error message or alert at this point if you wish, or leave it to be generated automatically.
9. Click OK.

Tip

Remember to save your work regularly.

Managing the database

Adding and deleting records

Adding a record or amending an entry is straightforward in both systems – the database application will automatically add a row to the table as you start to type into the bottom cell a spreadsheet has thousands of rows for you to use; and can grow whenever you need it to!

Deleting a record is a little trickier.

How to delete a record from the database

1. Click on the row indicator for the record you wish to delete.
2. Press Delete – you will be asked if you really want to delete the record.

Sorting

Sorting data into a particular order is the big advantage of using ICT over other database systems. If a customer asks for a particular laptop manufacturer, you can easily reorder your database to group all the records that have that manufacturer's name in them. If the customer then changes their mind, you can just as easily rerank your database. If they want to find a particular manufacturer *and* a particular option, such as **Bluetooth**, you can do that as well.

Both database and spreadsheet applications have a 'data filter' option.

How to sort data in a database application

1. In Table view, click in the cell that contains the data you want to search for and click on the Filter by selection button.
2. If you wish to add a second 'condition', click in another cell containing the relevant

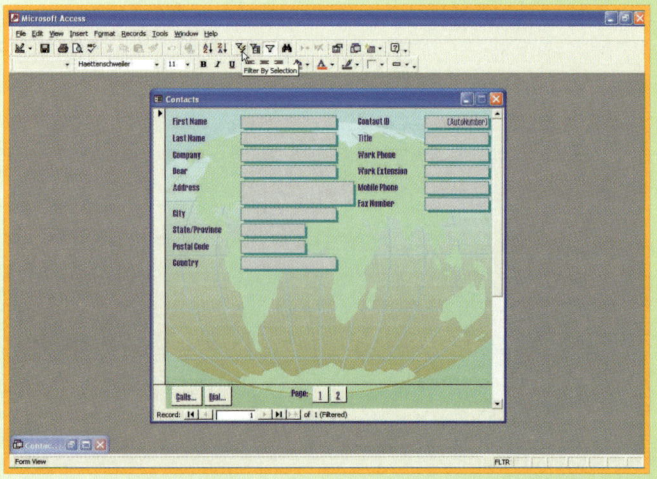

data and then click on the Filter by selection button again.

3 When you have finished or wish to start again, click on the Remove filter button.

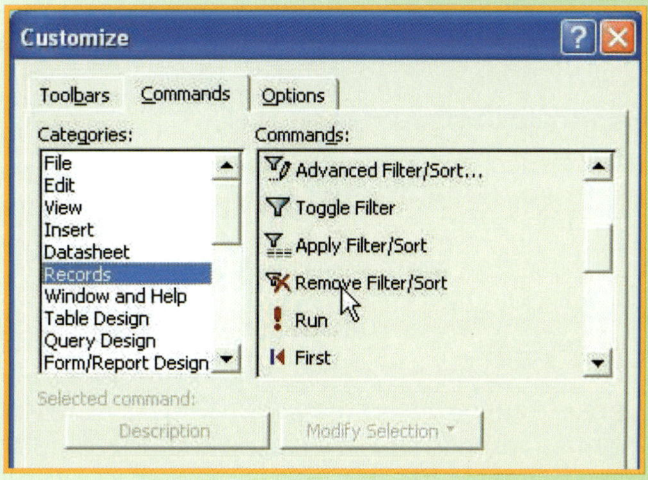

You can choose as many filters as you wish, but most databases can be searched easily with no more than three criteria.

Searching

To conduct a full search of your database is where the true database application starts to reveal why it is used.

If you went to a library you would not go to the enquiry desk and just ask for 'a book'. Before you start looking for something, you need some idea of what it is. In a spreadsheet all data is basically the same, but in a true database each piece of data is a separate entity – a field entry.

Let's go back to the original task – you were asked to design and build a database to store details about laptops. By using the sorting methods outlined above you would probably be able to find any particular piece of data for a customer regarding the purchase of a laptop. However, databases can be used for much more than this. As mentioned in Chapter 3, a database application can usually retrieve data and then produce a report. This report can then be used in other software to present the results from interrogating the data. Because of this extra level of functionality, the database application would normally be the software you choose to solve the task.

A database application allows you to develop complex queries and then run those queries against the data set. A query can be as simple as the filtering mentioned earlier:

'find me all the laptops that have DVD writer'

or it can involve **relational operators**:

'find me all the laptops with more than two USB2 ports'

or even **logical operators**:

'find me all the laptops that have a DVD writer, but do not have Bluetooth'.

To use these functions, you will need to build a query.

Queries

A query is a more accurate way of finding data in a database. This example will find the name and price of each laptop that has Bluetooth, has more than 512 MB RAM, is running Windows XP, but does not have a DVD writer.

Start by finding the query section of the application. You will notice that it also has a wizard – don't bother with it. Choose to create a query in Design view.

You are asked which table to use for the query. This is useful if you have more than one table, as in a relational database, but for this exercise you just need to make sure your table is highlighted and click Add, then close that dialogue box.

Now you can start to build your query. Start by choosing which field to look at first. You need the name and price, so they are your first choices – choose their fields from the drop-down lists. The 'Show' box is automatically ticked for you.

Then you need to build the query itself.

1. You need to know if it has Bluetooth – choose the Bluetooth field; you do not need to show it, so untick the 'Show' box; you need to add a criterion, in this case =yes (meaning, 'find me the fields that have a yes in them').
2. You need to know if it has more than 512 MB RAM – choose the RAM field, take off the 'Show' tick and add a criterion, >512 (meaning 'find me the fields that have numbers greater than 512 in them').
3. You need to know that it is running Windows XP – choose the field, take out the tick, add a criterion, =Windows XP.
4. You need to know that the machine does not have a DVD writer – choose the field, take out the tick, add the criterion, =no.

Then run the query, by clicking the ! (exclamation mark on the toolbar).

If the query does not give you what you want, return to the Design view and alter it accordingly. When it is doing what you want, save it with a specific name, for example, bt_512_xp_nodvd.

Relational operators and logical operators can be worked with in a spreadsheet, but it is a lot more complicated. If you have developed a database in a spreadsheet application and then find that you need this higher level of functionality, save the spreadsheet and then import the data into a database application – the basic structure is the same. The ability to exchange data so easily between applications is a very useful function, which we will come back to in a while.

Reporting

Getting a result from a query or filter is one thing, but being able to present it to someone else is an important aspect of using data. Most databases have a specific tool for generating reports. In this case it again offers two options: Design view or wizard. In this case the wizard is the easier option, so choose that.

1. The first dialogue box asks you to choose what to report on. If you want the whole data table, then choose your table from the drop-down menu, but usually you would only report on a specific part of the table – the results from a query.
2. To produce a report for a customer that gives them the result from the previous query, you would need to select the query name from the drop-down menu (now it becomes more obvious why particular names are chosen). There will only be the fields available that you have chosen to show in the query, so if you want to view more details you will need to go back and alter your query.
3. Select the fields that you want to show in your report and click Next.
4. Choose what order the fields will be shown in and click Next.
5. If there are lots of possible results to be shown, you may want to rank them. This is where you would choose to do this. Click Next.
6. The next option is to set the layout. As this is a small data set and a very small report, choose Columnar. Click Next.
7. The last selection is style – this depends on who your audience will be. Choose a style and click Next.
8. Now name the saved report and preview it.

Hopefully your report shows the data that your customer required and in an appropriate format. If it needs adjusting, select Design (Alt D) from the toolbar and adjust the design. Keep previewing as you adjust it.

> Dear Customer
>
> We have found a <manufacturer name> laptop that costs <price>. It seems to fit your requirements perfectly.
>
> Yours...

A final aspect of data manipulation is taking the data and using it for another purpose. The ability to import and export data is a great advantage in modern software. Being able to export the results of a query into a different application could be really useful.

The query above has reported a number of specific items from a database. This information could now be used in a word-processed letter to the customer.

How to insert data from a database into a word-processing program

1. Select the report you wish to use and right-click. Choose Export (or Alt F, Shift E) and navigate to where you want to save the data.
2. Choose a suitable file type – usually a spreadsheet, as it holds the data in an easily read format.
3. Save the report with a name you will remember.
4. Then load the word processor and follow the mail merge instructions (see page 33).
5. When it gets to 'Select the data source', navigate to the report you have saved and it will then link the data to the letter.
6. Type your letter, leaving appropriate spaces for the merge fields (the data from your report).
7. Enter the merge fields into the letter and then preview.

If it is all as you expected, then save the letter and run the merge. Usually you have the option to run the merge directly to the printer, or to the screen. If you intend to print a copy, then merging to the printer is obviously the option you need, but only choose that when you are certain that the merge has met your requirements.

Homework

1 Work through the database task, using your own field structure, and record 20 laptops. Produce a report for three different customers, requiring three different specifications for their laptops.

2 Carry out a similar exercise for a mobile phone database. Produce a report and merge it with a word-processed document that tells a prospective customer why a particular phone is the right one for their lifestyle.

3 Who do you know that uses a database? Teachers and lectures do. If you use the Internet you may be using a simple database to check for availability of an item, or by using names or part numbers on a website. Make a list of the uses of databases in everyday life.

CHAPTER 14

Email

What you will learn in this chapter

- You will learn about email in general.
- You will learn about email security.
- You will learn how to set up an email account.

Email software is used to send text messages, images, music, movies and any other type of file you can attach to them, to anyone, anywhere around the world. You can only send emails to a person who has an email address. Email addresses usually have a **name**, an @ symbol and the **name of the service provider**, for example:

dida is the only part that changes; the rest is the same for everyone who uses that service provider.

Service provider

dida@hotmail.co.uk

Your name

A very popular free way of getting email is to subscribe to a free email company such as Microsoft *Hotmail*® or Google™'s excellent advanced *Google Mail*. If you follow the easy-to-use online form you can soon start to send emails and pick them up from a computer anywhere in the world. To do this you need to access the right page for getting your emails and sign in using a password.

Most email addresses are free: there are dozens of Internet service providers who make money from them by offering the free service and using it as a means to send advertisements called junk mail.

The advantages of using email are that you can send just about any electronic file and it really is almost instant. Email saves money: no paper is needed, there are no phone call charges, no postage, no energy to deliver the information other than the power on your PC (although you should bear in mind that a dialup connection will charge you for the amount of time you are online).

Table 14.1 compares email with the traditional postal mail.

Table 14.1 Comparing email and postal mail

Email	Postal mail
You can use a keyboard to type an email message in an email program on your computer	You use a pen to write a letter on paper
When the letter is finished you press the send button in the email program	When the letter is finished you put it in an envelope, put a stamp on it and post it in a postbox
Emails are not delivered to the recipient directly, but wait on the nearest mail server for the recipient to pick them up	Letters are delivered to the recipient's door
Your email program can check for new email messages at your mail server and download them for you	If you have new mail in your mailbox you go and fetch it to read

Using email software

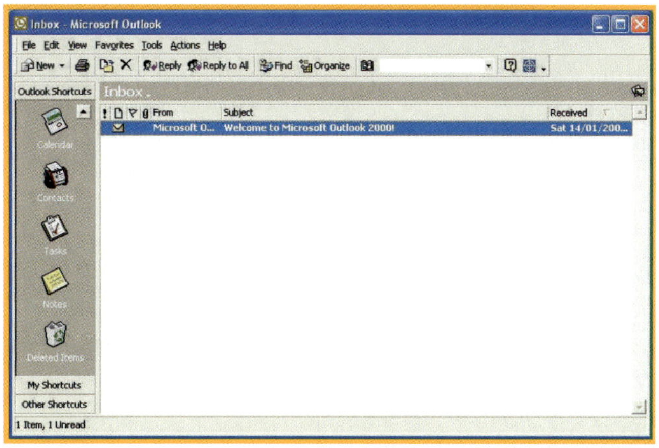

A typical email program is Microsoft *Outlook Express* ®. This usually comes with *Windows* ® software and is the most common program of this type. It allows you to receive and send emails, save addresses and has other facilities such as a spellchecker and formatting options. Other free web-based email services can give everybody in your household their personal email account; you can access your mail from almost every computer and it is free.

What can you do with email? You can:

- Write new letters
- Receive new letters
- Attach files and send them
- Receive and send images
- Receive and send sound files
- Receive and send movie clips.

Creating an email account

Web-based email services are normally free and allow you to access a personal mail account from anywhere on the planet where you can access the Internet. They normally have space for lots of messages to be kept. Some of the most popular email providers are listed below:

Google Mail – this is the service provided by Google, the search engine people – see gmail.google.com

Yahoo! – another search engine company. See www.yahoo.co.uk and click on the Mail icon at the top of the screen.

Hotmail – this service is provided by Microsoft® and is available at www.hotmail.com

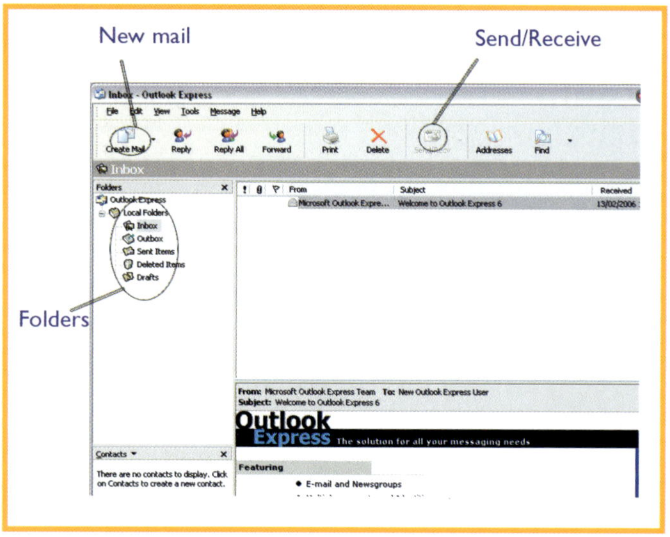

You can register with any of these mail providers and have your own email account running in minutes.

Sending and receiving email

Sending an email is easy. Once you have written your message and you have the email address of a friend to send it to, simply click on Send. When it comes to receiving emails, your service provider will store any that are sent to you, 24 hours a day, and when you next log on to your account will automatically download them so you can read them.

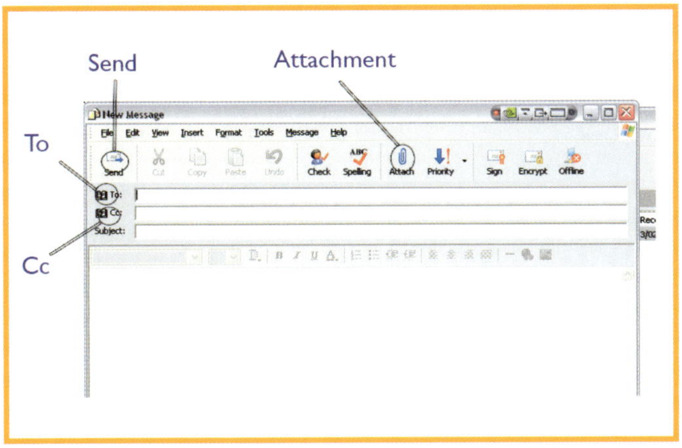

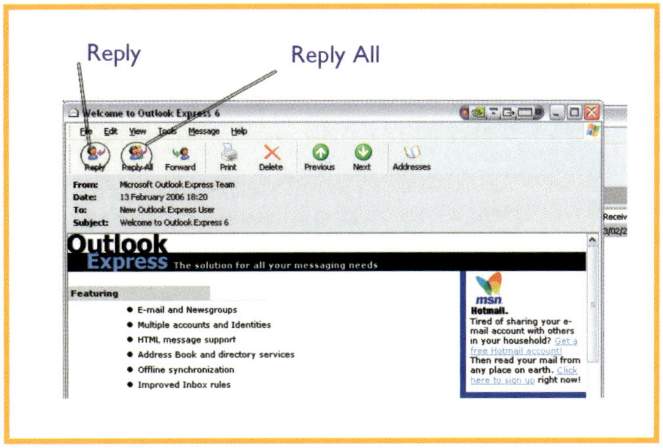

How reliable?

Email is extremely reliable, considering how many people use it, and rarely do messages go astray. However, sometimes the mail servers have problems. These are the machines that collect and send your email to the various other servers around the world. Unfortunately, systems can go wrong. Sometimes it is a software problem that can be fixed remotely, but sometimes it is a hardware problem. That may take some time to fix.

Spam

Spam is junk email. It is sent from addresses you do not recognise and normally contains adverts or offensive material. They can overwhelm your inbox if too many are sent. The best way to avoid spam is not getting on spammers' address lists in the first place.

Using your email address anywhere on the web puts it at risk of being picked up by spammers. Once an email address is in the hands of a spammer, your inbox will fill with spam every day.

When you sign up or leave your details for something on the web, there is often a box with some text beside it reading something like: 'Please pass my name on to selected third parties concerning products I might be interested in.' The box next to that text may already by ticked and if you do not untick it your email address will be given to third parties.

Everyone needs to be careful when giving their email address out!

Email netiquette

Emails have rules about what is considered polite and what is not polite, just like everyday conversations – email users refer to this set of rules as netiquette. Netiquette is well worth remembering because someone who receives an email from you cannot tell if you are smiling or laughing. So if you say something inappropriate, meaning it to be taken as a joke, the person you have emailed might interpret the message in the wrong the way and become offended. You need to think how you can send a message to say exactly what you want it to.

The golden rules of netiquette are:

- Make your email clear and easy to understand.
- Never send an email you would not like to receive.
- If you are replying to a message, try to use information from the original message.
- Try not to make jokes that could be misinterpreted.
- Sarcasm does not work on emails.
- Being rude to people on emails usually increases negativity.
- Sometimes you want to share emails with others. When forwarding emails, remember that the sender's email address will appear beneath your message on the email. Make sure that the sender is happy for their email address to be transmitted in this way, and that the original sender is happy for people to know what they wrote!
- Remember, not everyone is on **broadband**, so huge files containing pictures or movies could hold up their machines for ages.
- Certain file types can be confusing for people (some people will not know how to open Adobe *Acrobat* files or WinZip files, for example). Unless you are sure the person you are sending to has the right knowledge and software to open the files you are sending, it may be best to stick to more commonly available applications like Microsoft *Word*®.
- WRITING IN CAPITALS OR **bold text** can look like you are 'shouting', so try to avoid this.

Signing up to email

There are many companies offering free and safe email services that you can use. The world's most popular is MSN *Hotmail*®, which you can set up on the Internet and access all over the world. You simply log on to the *Hotmail*® site (www.hotmail.com) and fill out the form provided. Remember to make your password safe but easy to remember. Often you will find your name has already been taken by somebody else with the same name, so you might have to add numbers, letters or other characters to create a unique email address for yourself. For example, DaveParry@hotmail.com might already be taken, but Dave_Parry@hotmail.com (with an underscore) or DaveParry2006@hotmail.com might be available.

Google's *Google Mail* is becoming very popular and it is free to set up. To log on, go to Google (www.google.co.uk) and follow the *Google Mail* instructions. *Google Mail* allows you to retain huge amounts of emails and the amount is growing daily. So for saving images and important files its an extra safety net provide.

Email safety

Emails are wonderful to get and are similar to letters – they keep you in touch and help share information, linking friends and helping with work. Email can be a very safe way to communicate, but you need to use your common sense. A new email from someone you do not know may be from a boy or girl or long-lost relative, but it could be from a lunatic! So never agree to meetings or give out your full name, address or phone number, or any other personal information. If you are receiving nuisance emails, change your email address or use a function like the Block Sender option in MSN *Hotmail*® (most email accounts offer a similar function). You should also let a parent, teacher or other adult know that you have been receiving nuisance emails.

Unlike phone numbers, emails are not listed – there are too many and they are spread across the world. However, you may find a friend's email address if you go to www.bigfoot.com.

Tip

To avoid viruses infecting your computer and ruining your work, do not open attachments from sources you do not know, even if they are offering you something free or 'replying' to a message you do not remember sending.

How to change your email settings on Outlook Express

1 Open the *Outlook Express* ® program.

2 On the menu across the top, click on **Tools**.

3 Then click on **Accounts**.

4 Select **Mail Tab**.

5 Click on the email account you would like to change, then **Properties**.

6 Go to the General tab. Under User Information you can Change the User Name and other settings.

Netscape

1 Open Netscape's Message Centre

2 Choose the Preferences option from the Edit menu at the top of the screen.

3 Choose Identity from the Mail and Groups menu (left hand side of the screen)

4 You will find a section marked 'your name' on the right hand side: you can click on to it to change what is written there.

Homework

1 Log on to the web and sign up for an email address. Most school and college students should have a school one at least. When you have subscribed, send yourself an email to see how long it takes to arrive. Check with your teacher or other responsible adult that this is all right to do.

2 Type your name into a web browser and see what comes up. You may be surprised!

3 Look at the storage different email providers offer and list which gives you the most space.

4 Try to create an email group for your family and friends. Once you have located the group option, try inserting names from the address book.

CHAPTER 15

Internet and intranets

What you will learn in this chapter

In this chapter you will learn how the Internet came about and how to use it efficiently. There is a lot of jargon associated with the Internet and some of this is explained.

The Internet

The Internet is a huge network of computers. In fact, it is a huge network of networks. Every computer that logs on to the Internet does so through some sort of provider – this gateway is the link from one network to all the others.

The Internet came into being shortly after the Second World War, when a group of scientists who had been working together during the war decided to keep in touch and continue to work collaboratively. This small group worked in different institutions, mostly in the USA, and they linked the primitive computer systems of their workplaces together over the telephone system. Sixty years later there are over 580 million people using the Internet!

The Internet is simply a network: what makes it useful is the data that is transported through that network.

Intranets

Intranet systems are basically 'closed' networks that run exactly as the Internet does, the only difference being that they are not open to the public. To a user there is rarely any noticeable difference in the way an intranet system functions compared to the Internet.

Sometimes an intranet system is confined to a geographical area, such as a town, but often it is kept within a company premises. There are a number of intranets that can be accessed from anywhere, but they usually require the user to have a password and to log in.

If the Internet is the road system, an intranet is a private road network where only people with permission are allowed to drive. They use the same cars and obey the same Highway Code, but do not mix with the rest of the drivers.

Intranets are really useful where private and confidential material needs to be transferred over a network or use needs to be monitored, as in a school network. To use the example of the road system: a closed road system is a good place to test a new car, where the public will not be able to see it. It is also a good place to check how often a driver exceeds the speed limit!

Most schools and most large organisations have intranets, and some have developed **extranets** – a word that has recently come to mean an intranet system that can be accessed remotely through a standard Internet connection.

The World Wide Web

The most commonly used part of the Internet is the **World Wide Web** – www. This is the system that can deliver images, text, sound and video from anywhere in the world to any suitable computer. There are other systems that transmit data over the Internet, email for example, that are not part of the www system.

In order to have access to this massive resource, computers must have a common language. The language most commonly used is **HTML**, or Hypertext Markup Language. This is an electronic language that computers can understand. It uses a variety of words and instructions to communicate across the Internet.

There are other languages used to display information received from the Internet, such as Java and Lingo, but these are usually delivered by an HTML page, a bit like a jam doughnut – the jam comes inside the doughnut. Although the two materials are completely different, it would be very difficult to transport the jam without the doughnut (some might add that the doughnut is the dull bit and the jam the bit that is more fun, to continue the analogy!).

To view the programming language that a web page has been built in when viewing it in a browser window, click on View > Source (Alt V, Shift c).

Browsers

For a computer to be able to understand any of these languages it must have an application installed that can code and decode the data, a **browser**.

Browsers come in a variety of types; by far the most common is Microsoft *Internet Explorer* ®, an application developed as part of the *Windows*® system. But there are others. For PCs, *Firefox* and *Opera* are becoming more popular. For AOL, users have their own system. On Macs there are also different browsers: *Safari*, *Internet Explorer*® and *Firefox* are all popular.

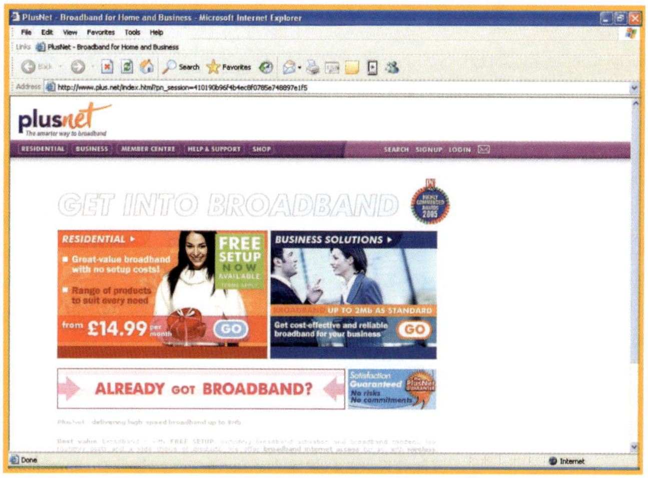

Whichever system is used, the principle is the same – the electronic data stream transmitted over the Internet is decoded via a **modem** into a programming language, HTML, and passed to the browser application.

The browser can translate the HTML into a page that can be shown on the screen for you to view.

Modern browsers can handle a wide variety of file types and media, through the addition of **plug-ins**. These are small bits of programs that are added to the browser application. You could think of them as foreign language dictionaries. The browser uses the plug-in to translate the code of a particular file type, as a person would use a foreign language dictionary to translate a word or sentence.

Modem

MODulator DEModulator – a piece of hardware that can decode the electrical signals that travel over the telephone lines

Addresses

To be able to access information over the Internet you need to know where it is! If you walk into a library and ask the librarian for 'a book' you will probably be laughed at! If you were to ask for a book about dinosaurs, you could be directed to a range of books, but it would be even better if you ask for a particular book, by a particular author.

If you want a precise piece of information you need to be able to ask a direct and accurate question – 'Could you tell me, what is the third word, on the fifth line, of the last page of *Romeo and Juliet*, please?' The librarian can then provide exactly what you require.

The Internet is just like a massive library. It has pages covering every subject you can imagine, from aardvarks to zebras and everything in between. To make sure you have a fruitful time on the Internet you must be prepared. Make sure you know what you want or where you can find it.

Every website has an address – a ***URL* (universal resource locator)**. This is like a household address and is made up from particular strings of data. If you can understand how they are made up, you stand a better chance of using them efficiently.

Take the address http://www.learn2.co.uk/dida as an example.

This is made from a number of elements:

- http:// stands for **hypertext transfer protocol** – this is the system used by the Internet to let the browser know that it will be receiving **hypertext** pages.
- www. – this tells the web server (the application running on the Internet servers) that the files to be shown will be public files, not intranet files.
- learn2 – this is a **domain name**. It is usually a name that has been purchased and registered by an individual, a company or an organisation. This is the name of the top level of the file structure where the web server will look for the requested pages.
- .co.uk – this is a suffix available for companies based in the UK. There are lots of others: .com is the most common as it relates to companies that can be based anywhere. The suffix, or extension, .gov.uk is used by sites that are government run, ac.uk is for colleges, and .sch.uk is for schools, and so on.
- dida – this slash, followed by a name, directs the web server to look in the subdirectory named 'dida'.

The web server will automatically follow the direction given by the URL and then look for a page with the title index or home, usually with a file type suffix of htm (abbreviated from html). If it finds a page with the correct name, it will then grab the data and return it to the browser. The browser will translate the code and rebuild the web page, as it was designed to look.

If the URL contains an error then the web sever will not be able to find the correct page and the browser will not be able to show the expected result.

Browser controls

As with all applications, a browser has a **GUI (graphical user interface)** that is designed to make most operations straightforward to carry out, usually with only a few clicks of the mouse.

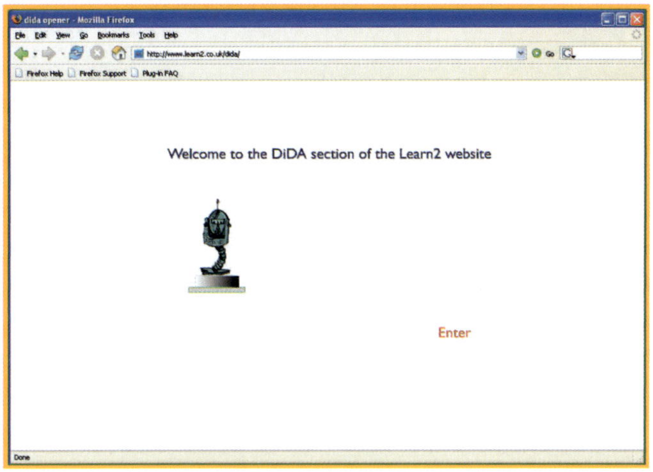

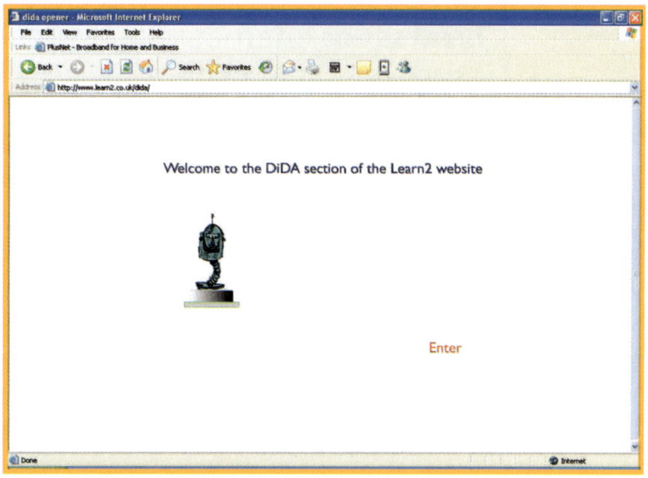

Internet Explorer® and *Firefox* have almost identical functions. The title bar at the top of the browser window gives the title of the page you are viewing and contains the minimise, maximise and close buttons.

The menu bar contains File, Edit, View, Tools and Help links. There are also links to what *Internet Explorer*® calls 'Favorites' (note the American spelling) and Firefox and other browsers call 'Bookmarks'. These are the same thing – they are URLs recorded in the browser memory, for future reference. Most of the menu commands are the same across the different browsers, as they are designed to do the same job – display web pages. The buttons on the toolbars also carry out the same operations, although they may look slightly different (Table 15.1).

Table 15.1

Description
Back – return to the page you viewed immediately prior to the one showing in the browser.
Forward – go forward to the page you have just gone 'back' from.
Stop – stop whatever is happening; useful if you have clicked something by mistake.

Refresh – pages can be loaded incorrectly, or information can be updated without the browser getting the updates; by clicking Refresh the request is sent to the web server to get the latest version of the page.
Home – the page that is shown when the browser starts, the home page. It can be set to any URL, but usually starts as something to do with the browser or Internet service provider (ISP). On an intranet system this is usually a log-in page.
Search – gives you access to a *search engine.*
Bookmarks/Favorites – gives you access to the URLs stored by the browser.
History – records every URL that the browser displays; useful if you find something and then need to go back to the source at a later time or date.
Email – as email uses the same infrastructure as the Internet, it is possible to send or receive emails while browsing.
Print – it is sometimes useful and necessary to print a web page; but bear in mind that web pages are not all the same size, or A4, so always preview before printing.

Web pages

The very nature of HTML and the other web-based languages is that the pages themselves can be designed to be 'dynamic'. A printed page from a book is flat: it can be read, but that is the limit of its functionality. A web page can look like a page from a book, but it can do so much more. It may contain a variety of different media:

- Text – typed text, formatted as it would be in a word-processed document
- Images – photographic quality pictures, manipulated to be appropriate for viewing on the screen
- Vector images – shapes and colours used to enhance the appearance of the page
- Animated video clips using vector graphics
- Full motion video
- Sound
- Games

and just about anything else that can be transmitted electronically.

But even this is only like watching a television as opposed to reading a book – it is just as flat. What makes websites potentially more interesting is the ability to interact with what is going on using interactive components, such as forms, buttons and **hyperlinks**.

Any part of a web page can be turned into a **hyperlink**. Often this is associated with text, but it can be anything: text, images, animation or a combination.

When you move your mouse pointer over the hyperlink the browser detects it and then carries out a function set within the code of the web page. For example, moving the pointer over a small image can make it grow so that you can see it more clearly. This type of 'rollover' is commonly used on buttons; as the pointer rolls over the button it changes its appearance, making it stand out from the rest of the page, and therefore making it more likely that the user will press it!

This is a simple operation. A more complicated rollover is where you move the mouse pointer over a particular area of the screen and something happens in another part – this is called a **disjointed rollover**.

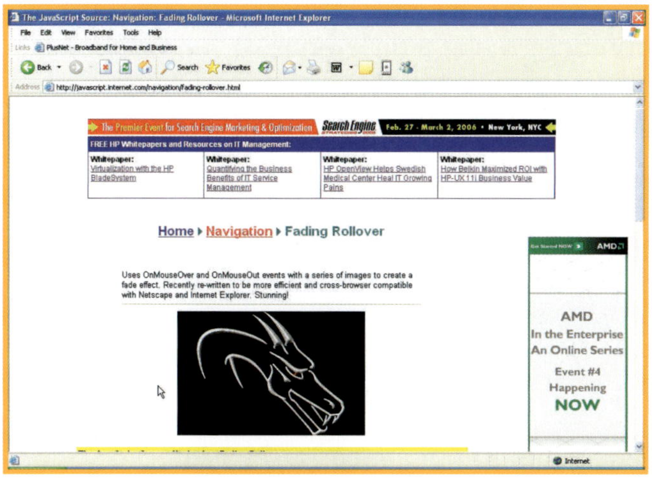

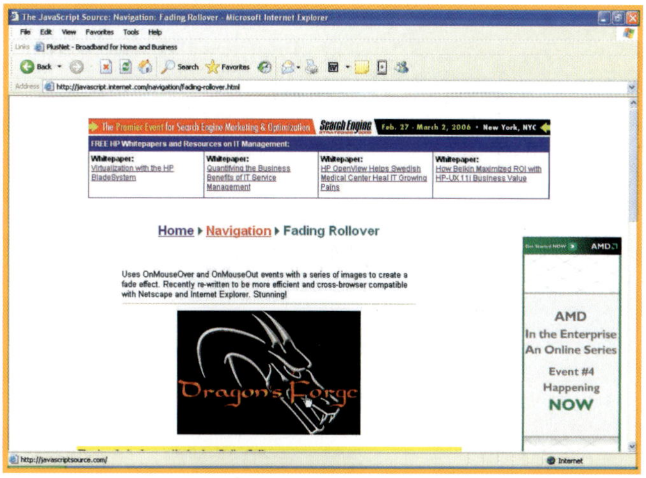

Both these examples show that the browser can capture movement. By clicking buttons on the screen you can also make the browser carry out a particular task, such as moving you to another part of the web page or opening another website.

Data capture

The ability of a web page to capture movement and action can be taken further through the use of forms. A form can be built into a web page. When a user completes it, the data is then captured by the browser and can be sent to the web server.

In this way, web-based materials can become truly interactive. The response the user makes on the web page can be captured and sent to the web server, which can then, automatically, search for a subsequent page and deliver that back to the user. This can make every user have a different experience on the same website. This function also enables web pages to run searches.

Searching

Whether you choose to search using the toolbar on the browser, or by going to a search page on a website, you are accessing the same functionality. A search carried out by a web browser works in exactly the same way as a search on a database or spreadsheet. You enter the search criteria and the web browser sends the request to a web server. The web server then carries out the search, using specialist software.

As with searching a database, or running a query, the more detail you can add to the search criteria, the more likely it is that you will get a good result.

If you want to find the price of a new Ford car in Essex, you should include a number of words, in your search perhaps:

Ford new Essex

Capitalisation is irrelevant, but punctuation does make a difference. A full stop means 'and' so if you want to search for all three words, use full stops between 'Ford' and 'new', and 'new' and 'Essex':

ford.new.essex

This makes the **search engine** look for a web page containing 'Ford' *and* 'new' *and* 'Essex'. It will not return a page that has only 'Ford' and 'Essex'.

There are other tricks to help organise your searching:

- + in front of a word means 'is required'
- – in front means 'is not required' (meaning it must not appear in the result)
- quotation marks will restrict the search to finding exactly what appears inside the quotes
- * (asterisk) can be used as a 'wildcard', standing in for letters or words when you are unsure of what might be in the search criteria. For example, d*ve will make the search look for words that have 'd v e', and the second letter can be any letter of the alphabet.

Search engine
The term used to describe the software that runs a search from a web browser

There is a variety of different search engines, some of which specialise in particular areas of interest. The most popular general search engine at the moment is Google (www.google.co.uk), but also popular are Ask Jeeves (www.ask.co.uk) and LIxquick (www.ixquick.com).

There are online telephone directories (for example, www.192.com), Business directories (for example, www.scoot.co.uk) and all manner of others. Try entering 'specialist search engines' into one of those mentioned earlier!

Saving and printing

When you have found the page you were after, and it shows the information that your search requested, you will want to do something with it.

If you think you may need to come back to it at a later date, rather than using the 'history' function you could save the URL in your Bookmarks or Favorites. This stores the URL and puts a hyperlink in your folder that you can click on to open the page.

You can also save the page 'for offline use'. If you do this, a copy of the page is taken and stored in your temporary files so that you can access it through your Favorites/Bookmarks in the same way, but it will not be updated if the 'real' page changes. You may want just part of the page, in which case you could copy the particular section, as you would with any other document, and paste it into a word-processed document. However, this will normally only copy the standard HTML of the page. Anything like video or sound may be lost, as will much of the interactivity.

Copying and pasting is probably the most useful way to collect information from a site for use in your own work, as you can quickly gather small 'chunks' of useful data. But you must remember to record where you got it from, so that you can acknowledge it in your own materials. This is also a good method of building up a page for printing, as web pages are often odd sizes and printing the original page can be problematic. If you must print the web page as it is, preview it first. If it seems that part of it is not going to print, it may be possible to do a screen grab (Alt and Print Screen) and then paste the screen grab into a document.

Homework

1. Carry out a web search to investigate the history of the Internet. Produce a timeline of the developments that have led to the Internet as it is today.
2. View the HTML behind the web page www.learn2.co.uk. See if you can work out when the site was built.
3. Investigate the Edexcel site (http://dida.edexcel.org.uk/home).

4 Use a search engine to gather a range of useful DiDA sites and record them in your Favorites/Bookmarks for future reference.

5 You should be aware of Internet security and personal safety issues. Check with your school or college for information and try a web search too.

CHAPTER 16

Presentation software

What you will learn in this chapter

- You will learn how to build a Microsoft *PowerPoint* ® presentation and how to avoid producing a poor slide show.
- Detailed skill sections show you the basics of using Microsoft *PowerPoint* ® software and how to relate the slide show to the target audience.

Presentation software, such as Microsoft *PowerPoint* ®, is designed to present information to an audience. The design and feel of the presentation should always match the audience's needs. Projection of Microsoft *PowerPoint* ® presentations is commonplace today and usually means that the work is designed for big screens. However, this is not always the case.

Presentation software is very powerful and is used in industry for many reasons, for example, to train, educate or persuade people to sign up to something or to buy a product. It can also be used as a learning tool and to display data to an audience, using Microsoft *Excel* ® graphics and charts.

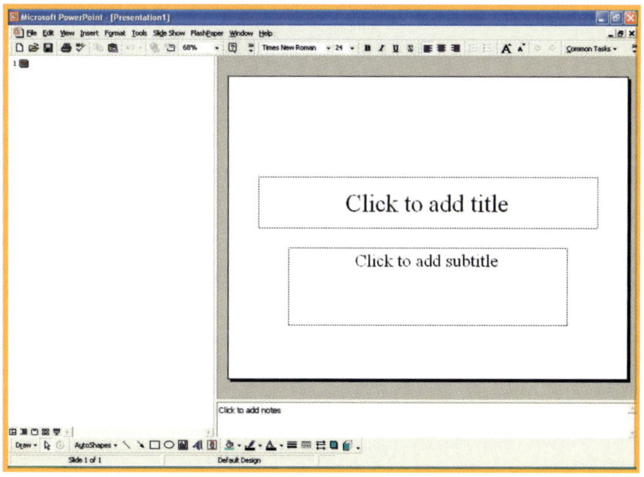

With this type of software application you will find a range of tools to help you design unique presentations. There are also ready-made backgrounds or formatted pages you can use that allow you to work at speed on a pre-designed theme. These are called templates.

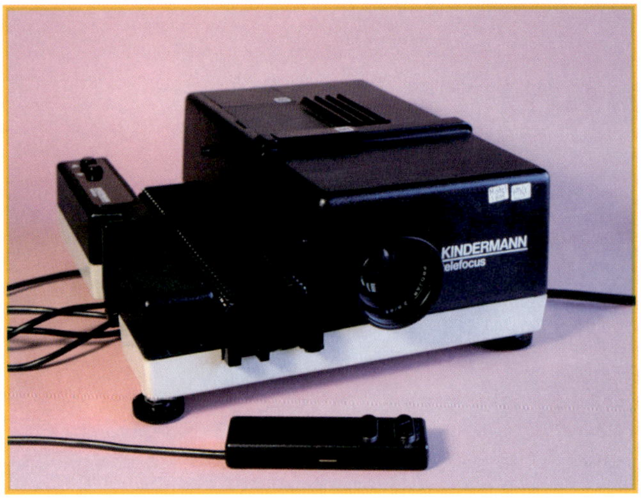

Figure 16.1

Pages in presentation software are usually called slides. In the past, presentations were based on photographic slides and slide projectors. These slides had to be developed in a darkroom. The slides were inserted into the projector manually and had no flexibility as they were fixed images. Text was difficult to place on slides, as once again it had to be photographed onto a slide.

Presentation software can also produce animations and web pages. There are drawing tools, text tools the same as those found in Microsoft *Word*®, plus a range of animation tools. The animation tools allow you to create movement with text objects or images. Sometimes people overdo these. Although fun and interesting, animation overload can easily distract the audience from the points being made on a slide. You should use them as a *point maker* or to reinforce information to your audience. There is more on this topic on page 66.

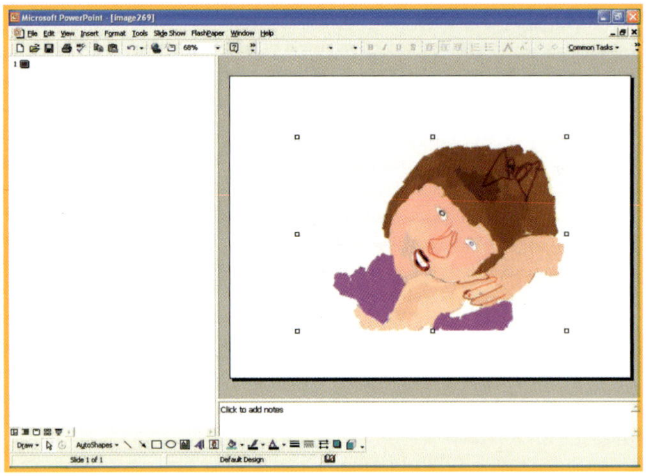

The tools in Microsoft *PowerPoint*® are very similar to those in Microsoft *Word*®, with the addition of the specialist presentation tools. These include sound, animations and slide transition tools. So if you are familiar with Microsoft *Word*®, you should find the tools and dialogue box layout straightforward.

With presentation software you can easily create slides that support your ideas in a visually appealing manner. Presentations can be in the form of a slide show that runs on your computer screen or is projected on to a screen, can be printed on to overhead transparencies or 35 mm transparencies, or can be run on a Microsoft *PowerPoint*® viewer or even on the Internet. Presentation software offers you the chance to show off your graphics skills, introduce speakers' notes, handouts, voice-overs, music, movies and animations. There are also many more options to customise a presentation.

Running a presentation

Think about the following considerations; these will enhance the effectiveness of your presentations.

Planning your presentation

Before you create your presentation, plan how you want to use the presentation and consider the following questions:

- What are your goals for the presentation?
- How can you enhance the understanding of the material?
- Is the content primarily text? If so, do not put too much on each slide.
- Will you use handouts to supplement the presentation?
- Can the information be divided into manageable 'chunks'?

You may want to use presentations to help understand notes, or present visual images to enhance the information you are trying to communicate.

Creating multimedia programs takes a lot of time, so consider using parts of products already on the market before creating your own presentation. There may be illustrations, photographs or video clips on a CD-ROM that you can incorporate into your presentation easily. However, before using any multimedia in a presentation, make certain you have copyright permission.

Setting out your presentation

The first slide in a presentation usually sets the scene for the rest: it should be general; then, as the slide show moves on, each slide should become more specific. Each of your slides should have enough information to cover one major point, which will then build up to a conclusion on the final slide. Details can be made easier to follow by using bullet points.

Slides should have key words to support the theme, but never long sentences or long blocks of text. Remember, you can add sound or music, or you can talk along as the slide show is played.

A slide show is never the same as a book – it is a method of conveying information in short bursts, supported by a range of additional media, if required. The slide show itself can sometimes be less important than the accompanying speech, so bear that in mind as a possible idea.

Help your audience by using titles and headings to keep the objectives clear. The first slide is probably the most important because it needs to catch the attention of your audience. Their attention should then be held with the rest. Your audience may be sitting down, in which case they are passive (not able to do much). As a result of this they need to have a relatively short presentation and 20 minutes or so is probably long enough. Good presenters may break up a presentation with a web link, a movie, a music section, an exercise for the audience, discussions or question-and-answer sessions.

The failure of a presentation is not usually a consequence of poor content, but more about the way in which it is presented. Too much animation, bad colour schemes, poor background, illegible text and too much text all contribute to a presentation faiing to achieve its purpose. By all means use animation, but try to restrict it to appropriate sections, perhaps to enhance a point or to liven up a dull section.

Preparing your presentation

Once you plan a presentation based on your goals, the presentation can be as low-tech or high-tech as your skills and equipment allow. Besides charts and clip art, new technology allows you to insert digital audio or video files.

Top tips

- Limit the use of serif types such as Times, Times New Roman or Palatino to headings or subheadings. The variations of thin and thick lines present problems for on-screen displays. Recommended fonts are Helvetica, Arial and AvantGarde.
- The above guidelines for font and colour also apply to charts and graphs. All titles and labels should be visible from the back of the room. For a clear image, avoid using three-dimensional effects.

Practice before you present, not only with the script and presentations, but also with all the equipment. You are relying on electrical equipment – a computer, projector, touch screen, extension leads and many other small parts that could fail. Would you be able to change a bulb or a fuse? Do you need a technical support team or person? What would you do if the power failed? I always carry a backup copy of my presentation in two places: one in a case, and one in my computer, I always double-check the movie and sound systems are working and I do this by getting ready early.

You will never feel confident unless you are well informed about your subject and are clear about what form the presentation will take. So go through it with a friend or your tutor until you are slick!

The physical size and lighting conditions of the room will affect your presentation. Make sure everyone can see the screen, that everyone has good lighting and that everyone can hear you and see you. Distribute copies of the presentation so that people can follow or take notes if they need to.

The time your presentation takes is decided by the content of each slide and the amount of time it takes for your audience to absorb the information. However, do allow the audience a reasonable amount of time to read the slides. You may need to emphasise important points and this may mean some slides are viewed for longer periods than others. This is where your testing comes in handy, as you can time a 'test audience' – consisting, perhaps, of your friends or tutors, and see how long it takes for them to finish reading and absorb the information presented in the slide show.

As Microsoft *PowerPoint*® slides can be uploaded to a website for future reference, this is an important point to make at the beginning and end of a presentation if this is what you have done. This could also save time and money on printing and distribution costs.

You can even create audio files to narrate your Microsoft *PowerPoint* ® presentation. This can be a very useful tool if you leave the presentation on the web.

Starting a new presentation

When you open Microsoft *PowerPoint* ®, you see the Start-up dialogue box (see opposite). You can choose from these options.

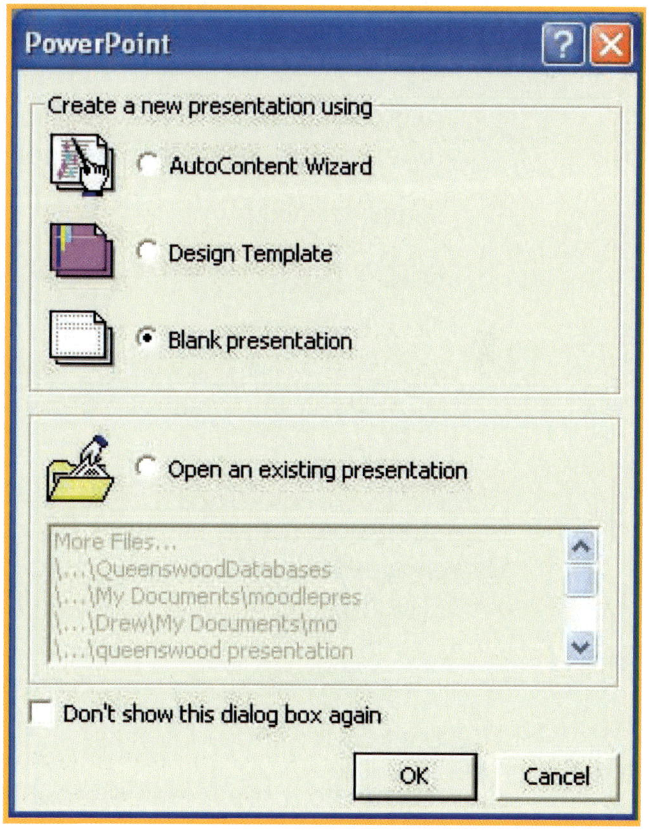

Starting a presentation

One of the main advantages of using Microsoft Office ® software is that a lot of the tools and their position on the screen are very similar. Microsoft *PowerPoint* ® has many of the features and tools found in Microsoft *Word* ® and *Excel* ®. Therefore, if you know how to use one, you only need to learn how to use the specialised features of the other. Although the tools are similar to Microsoft *Word* ®, Microsoft *PowerPoint* ® has the additional presentation features which can be used at any level. Microsoft *PowerPoint* ® has an auto content wizard that will run through an entire presentation, suggesting preset formats and allowing you to insert graphics. All you need to do is add your own content.

Templates are basically pre-planned pages which are usually designed for a specfic task. As a result, they can save time; however, you are really limited to someone else's ideas and you could probably do as well by starting with a new presentation and a blank page. Doing it yourself means that you have total control over what is seen, and in the process you can learn to use all the features of the software more quickly. Remember, your Microsoft *PowerPoint* ® presentations will probably take longer than you think to complete, so you should back up straightaway. As soon as you start your presentation, give your file a name and press Control S on the keyboard, or click Save, every few minutes. You should also back up to some sort of portable media.

To view your work

You can display your Microsoft *PowerPoint*® slides in five different ways:

1 Slide Sorter view

Shows the slides in miniature – you can use this for changing the order of slides by dragging and dropping.

2 Outline view

This view shows you bulleted text on the slides in outline format, with a small window showing one slide at a time. This is good for development purposes.

3 Slide view

Allows you to see only your slide to work on. This view shows you one slide at a time and would be the view you use when constructing and designing a slide.

4 Slideshow view

Allows you to view the finished design as the audience would see it.

5 Note page view

Shows a small view of your slide and an area for note making.

Opening a presentation

Sometimes we forget what the file name was and where it was saved. Microsoft *PowerPoint*® will find the file for you.

1. Go to Open.
2. Click Preview.
3. Look in the drop-down list and chose the drive letter: C, D, E, etc.
4. If you know the folder, choose it.
5. Search for content by clicking Command and settings in the open dialogue box.
6. Choose Search subfolders.
7. At the bottom of the dialogue box fill in the search box for a word you know was in the file.

8 Click Find Now and you will get a list of all the files with the words you specified in them.

Building a presentation

Adding slides

You construct a presentation by adding slides. Each slide has a basic structure, for example, whether it has text on it and where that text will go. This layout may also include space for graphics or a movie clip.

How to add a slide

1 Choose Insert > New Slide.

2 Choose an Auto Layout by selecting the picture of your preferred layout. When you click an Auto Layout, you will see a brief description of that layout.

3 When you find one you wish to use, click OK.

Applying a background

The backgrounds you choose for your presentation can mean the difference between success and failure. The wrong colour or texture can make viewing difficult or give the presentation the wrong feel. You can display backgrounds to your slide show by going to Format, Background.

You then have the same options as you would do in Microsoft *Word* ®: colour ranges, textures and fill effects. Simply choose the ones you need and either apply to one slide or to all of them.

Tip

Right-click the mouse over any toolbar and choose Common Tasks to display the Common Task toolbar where you can add new slides and layouts.

Text boxes

Using text boxes has several advantages, especially if you are designing your slides from scratch. The text box can be moved around the page with the text inside. Unlike words in a word processor, which can only be moved by the return or space bars, text boxes allow you to place text at any angle or stretched into a range of shapes. Text boxes can have a different colour from the background and have borders placed around them.

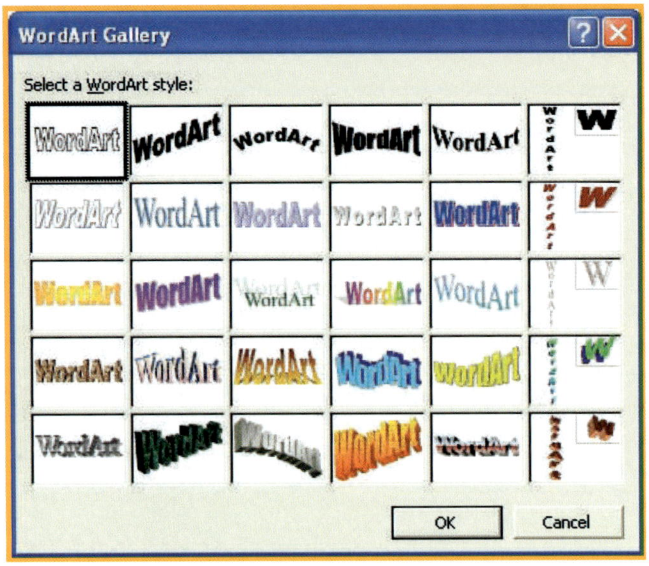

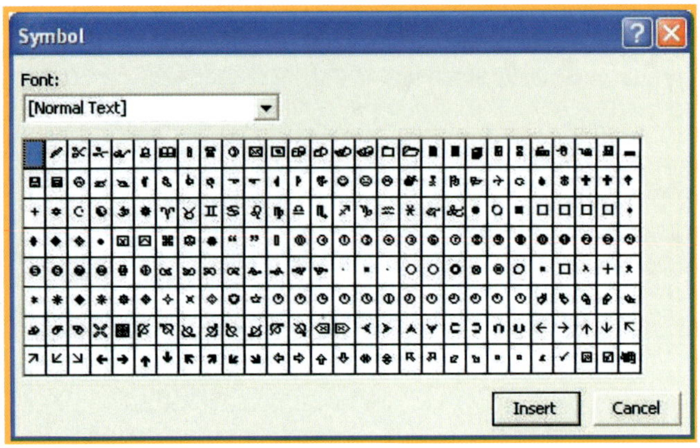

WordArt

WordArt is great fun and can be very useful, but be careful. WordArt text can be impossible to read if it is too distorted. It does have a place in presentations, but not as text or body type (the main text); instead it can be used to make fun titles and subtitles. WordArt works the same way in Microsoft *PowerPoint* ®, *Word* ® and *Excel* ®.

You simply click on the WordArt icon, select your shapes and type in your text. In the edit section you can type in your text over the dummy text, change fonts, size and style. WordArt text can be moved in the same way as text boxes, by clicking and dragging on the shaded edges until the crossed arrows appear, and then simply dragging it to the position required.

Symbols

The easiest way to place symbols is to look at the font called Wingdings – each letter on the keyboard is a symbol. These can be enlarged or placed into text boxes.

Homework

1 Select a template and try to follow the wizard's instructions to make a simple presentation. You choose the subject.

2 Design a slide using a serifed typeface, then copy it and change the font to a sans serif typeface. See if it makes any difference to your audience.

3 Use Sound Recorder in the Windows ® operating system to produce a simple sound file. Save this somewhere safe and load it into a Microsoft *PowerPoint* ® presentation. Show the slide and

see if the sound works. You can get it to work automatically or by clicking on the icon of a speaker.

4 Add two blank slides and try to link them through hyperlinked objects (boxes, circles, etc.). This will allow you to switch between the two slides in presentation mode.

5 Select a few pages and try to insert Action Buttons to link pages. Action Buttons are found in the Drawing toolbox.

CHAPTER 17

Spreadsheet software

What you will learn in this chapter

In this chapter you will learn how to use Microsoft *Excel* ® spreadsheet software to produce charts and work with data. The chapter also looks at other ways you can use Microsoft *Excel* ® creatively.

What is a spreadsheet?

Spreadsheets have existed in paper form for many years. Electronic versions on computers are a much more recent invention. A spreadsheet contains columns and rows of cells. Cells are boxes that can contain data, and allow this data to be manipulated in different ways. Spreadsheets are powerful tools and are used in businesses all over the world
.

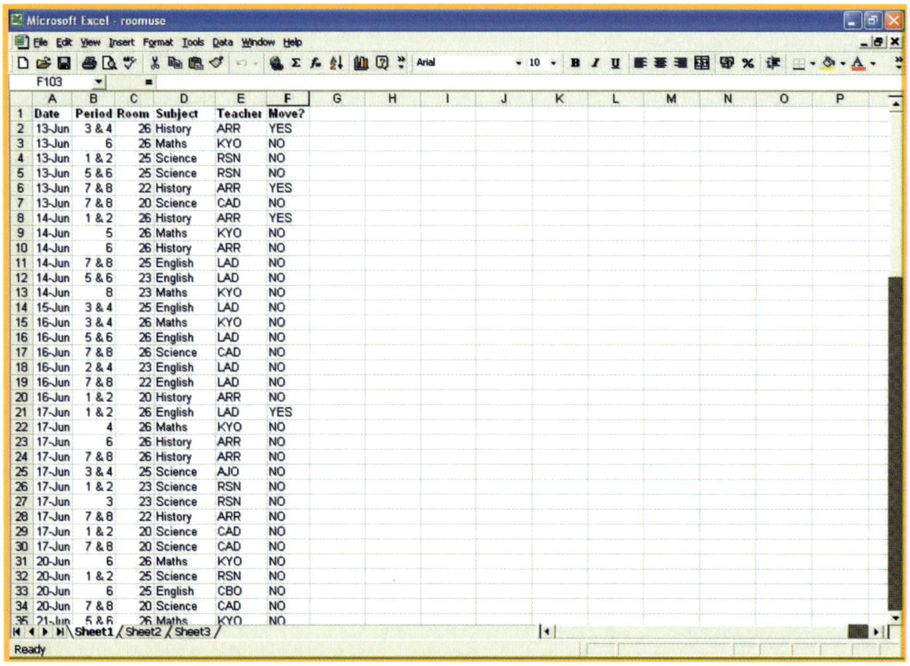

	A	B	C	D	E	F
1	Date	Period	Room	Subject	Teacher	Move?
2	13-Jun	3 & 4	26	History	ARR	YES
3	13-Jun	6	26	Maths	KYO	NO
4	13-Jun	1 & 2	25	Science	RSN	NO
5	13-Jun	5 & 6	25	Science	RSN	NO
6	13-Jun	7 & 8	22	History	ARR	YES
7	13-Jun	7 & 8	20	Science	CAD	NO
8	14-Jun	1 & 2	26	History	ARR	YES
9	14-Jun	5	26	Maths	KYO	NO
10	14-Jun	6	26	History	ARR	NO
11	14-Jun	7 & 8	25	English	LAD	NO
12	14-Jun	5 & 6	23	English	LAD	NO
13	14-Jun	8	23	Maths	KYO	NO
14	15-Jun	3 & 4	25	English	LAD	NO
15	16-Jun	3 & 4	26	Maths	KYO	NO
16	16-Jun	5 & 6	26	English	LAD	NO
17	16-Jun	7 & 8	26	Science	CAD	NO
18	16-Jun	2 & 4	23	English	LAD	NO
19	16-Jun	7 & 8	22	English	LAD	NO
20	16-Jun	1 & 2	20	History	ARR	NO
21	17-Jun	1 & 2	26	English	LAD	YES
22	17-Jun	4	26	Maths	KYO	NO
23	17-Jun	6	26	History	ARR	NO
24	17-Jun	7 & 8	26	History	ARR	NO
25	17-Jun	3 & 4	25	Science	AJO	NO
26	17-Jun	1 & 2	23	Science	RSN	NO
27	17-Jun	3	23	Science	RSN	NO
28	17-Jun	7 & 8	22	History	ARR	NO
29	17-Jun	1 & 2	20	Science	CAD	NO
30	17-Jun	7 & 8	20	Science	CAD	NO
31	20-Jun	6	26	Maths	KYO	NO
32	20-Jun	1 & 2	25	Science	RSN	NO
33	20-Jun	6	25	English	CBO	NO
34	20-Jun	7 & 8	20	Science	CAD	NO
35	21-Jun	5 & 6	26	Maths	KYO	NO

You will probably use a spreadsheet for creating graphs from data you have collected, perhaps from a survey or questionnaire. Spreadsheets are brilliant for displaying data graphically. The graphs can then be cut or copied and pasted into most other software, for example Microsoft *PowerPoint* ®, *Word* ®, web software, and so on.

An electronic spreadsheet such as Microsoft *Excel* ® organises information into software-defined **columns and rows**.

- Columns go up and down.
- Rows go across.

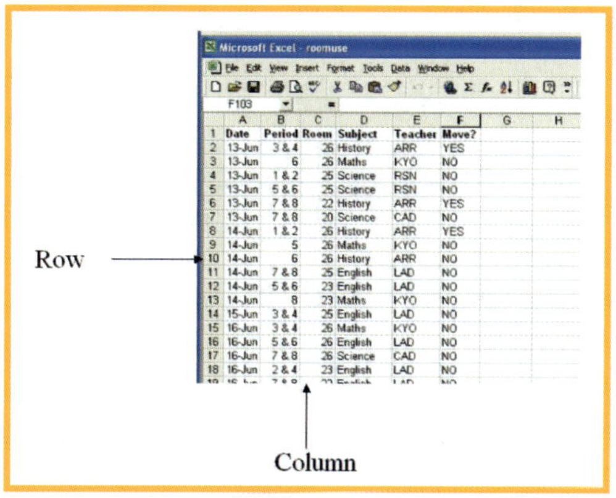

The data can then be 'added up' by a formula to give a total or sum. A spreadsheet application can summarise information from different sources and present the information in a particular format as the user requires. The data may be taken into Microsoft *PowerPoint* ® as part of a presentation.

Microsoft *Excel* ® allows you to build a 'Workbook'. This is a collection of spreadsheets: *Excel* ® calls them 'worksheets'. These worksheets can be independent of each other or linked.

Each worksheet can be huge – over 65,000 rows and 256 columns – more than you will probably need!

To summarise, Microsoft *Excel* ® software can be used for:

- Graphics
- Adding up
- Multiplying
- Subtracting
- Dividing
- Inserting images and text
- Displaying data via a presentation
- Making lists
- Sorting by size or alphabetically.

Working with graphics

The graphical possibilities that Microsoft *Excel* ® software offers are probably going to be well used in your DiDA course. They are easy to use and the results look very good.

The making of graphs from data is very straightforward and, providing you choose an easy-to-understand graph, it can make data much clearer.

Inserting graphics

You can insert three kinds of graphics into a Microsoft *Excel* ® document: a graphic file that you already have, clip art that comes with Microsoft Office ®, or AutoShapes that are also a part of most Microsoft Office ® programs (see below).

How to insert a graphic file

1. Choose Insert > Picture > From File.
2. Find the file you want to insert and select it.
3. Click Insert.

Tip

Insert a text box first. With the text box selected, insert the file.

Formatting in Microsoft *Excel* ®

Formatting has to do with setting text or backgrounds, fonts and colours. As we all seem to have colour screens and colour printers, we have a huge array of resources available to us. The problem with this is the same as the problems we mentioned with presentation software: people can get carried away with too many colours and too many fonts that become illegible.

You can use colour in Microsoft *Excel* ® to highlight columns by selecting the column on the top grey bar with a letter on it and dipping into the colour plaette. Selecting the grey letter boxes is a bit like highlighting text in word-processing documents – it informs the computer you wish to apply formatting to that selected area.

To align the text (make it centred or ranging to the right or left) is the same process as in word-processing.

Adding borders

Adding a border adds focus to your work on the Microsoft *Excel®* worksheet. To add a border, highlight your work by dragging the mouse from the top right to the bottom left of your work, then go to the formatting toolbar and find Borders. Here you will have a range of options to choose from. To add a colour click Fill colour on the formatting toolbar while your work is still highlighted.

Sometimes you may wish to make two or more cells into one – this is called merging. To merge cells, simply highlight the cells you wish to merge and click on Merge and Center on the formatting toolbar. This is always useful for creating title bars at the top of your worksheet.

Making a chart

If you have created a simple list of text with number values – perhaps the result of a survey – you may want to create a chart. We tend to call charts 'graphs', but because Microsoft *Excel®* is used throughout the world, the term 'charts' is used. The simple way to create a chart is to highlight your work, then click on Chart Wizard. Chart Wizard gives you a range of different charts to choose from. It is very important that you choose the right charts for your presentation or publication, so some thought should go into deciding which type is most appropriate. As you go through Chart Wizard you will be offered a range of text and graphics options. Choose these if you wish, or keep clicking on Next,then Finish, your chart will be presented to you in colour. Once you have your chart you can copy or cut it and paste it into any publication presentation package or web page.

Splitting frames

Sometimes your worksheet can become too big to see and will not fit on to one screen. This problem can be solved by splitting the worksheet into smaller, scrollable sections. To do this you simply go to Window, then click on Split and the worksheet will be divided up into four frames instead of the normal one.

Splitting frames may be useful when you are working on several pieces of work at the same time. The fames are all scrollable.

Printing your worksheets

To check how a sheet will look when printed, click on Print Preview.

To print out your worksheet and not the entire Microsoft *Excel®* sheet available, highlight the work you wish to print and choose Print Area.

Tip

The bit many beginners get wrong is that they do not leave an empty cell for the answer to go in, so always click in a cell directly below your numbers, or to the right of a row of numbers – this makes it the Active Cell.

Printed page setup

Here you can set pages to landscape or portrait, scale margins, and so on. In this area you can also select the option of printing the gridlines seen on the normal worksheet or removing them.

Microsoft *Excel* ® has a shortcut to make it easy to add rows or columns of figures together.

If you click on the sigma sign (this looks like an 'M' standing on its side) the answer to your formula, will appear in the first cell you highlighted (the empty one).

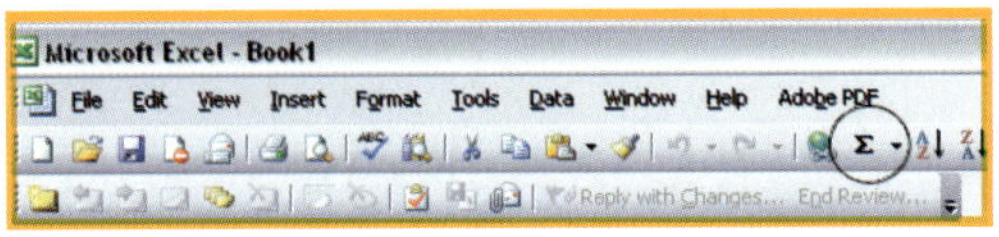

In Microsoft *Excel* ® formulas start with the equals sign (=), which can be found on the top right of your keyboard. This informs Microsoft *Excel* ® that you wish to enter a formula in the cell, and not a value or label. To do a simple sum you need to insert one of the following mathematical signs:

/ (slash) for division
* (asterisk) for multiplication
+ (plus sign) for addition
– (minus sign) for subtraction
% (percentage sign) for percentages.

You will notice that the symbols used are very similar to those you would use on paper calculation, except for the slash symbol, which is used for division.

Never include spaces in a formula as these will make the calculations fail.

If you wanted to multiply the contents of cell B3 by C3, this formula needs to start with = sign, then B3*C3 (this will give you =B3*C3).

To enter the formula:

1. Click in cell D3
2. Type the formula **=B3*C3**
3. Press Enter

Your answer will be shown in cell D3 and the formula will be shown in the formula bar on the top of the spreadsheet. With all formulas, always state the column first, then the row, for example, D4 is column D and row 4.

Once you have entered the formula **=B3*C3** in cell D3, Microsoft *Excel*® will calculate the answer, based on the values currently in the cells; if you change the values, *Excel*® will automatically recalculate the formula using the new values.

The AutoSum quick route

The AVERAGE formula can be done in the following way:

1. Type a few numbers in a column.
2. Remember to click the cell directly below the numbers to make space for the answer.
3. Then type = and then **AVERAGE**, followed by brackets containing the first cell reference, a colon and the last cell reference to be included.
4. Press Enter on the keyboard.

Relative references

Microsoft *Excel*® formulas use relative referencing – this is done by default. If it is a **relative** reference, if you copy the formula into another cell, the formula will apply to new cells. For instance, if cell A3 contained the formula **=A1+A2**, then if you copied cell A3 to cell B3, cell B3 would now contain the formula **=B1+B2**.

Absolute references

Absolute references will never automatically change, even if copied or moved. They reference the same cell address, no matter where the formula is in the spreadsheet. Absolute references are shown by the dollar ($) sign preceding the row or column designation that is absolute. For example A1 + A3 will make A1 an absolute cell reference.

Viewing your spreadsheet efficiently

Spreadsheets can get very big, too big to fit on your screen at the same time. You need to know how to navigate as well as some special viewing tricks.

- *Using the* **scroll bars**: You can use the vertical and horizontal scroll bars to move around your spreadsheet.
- *Using keyboard shortcuts*: Table 17.1 shows some useful shortcuts.

Table 17.1 Keyboard shortcuts in Microsoft *Excel* ®

To:	Press:
Move one cell in a given direction	Arrow key
Move to the edge of the current data region (an area where you have put data that is surrounded by space or borders) Move one cell to the right	Ctrl+ arrow key Tab
Move to the beginning of the row	Home
Move to the beginning of the worksheet, usually A1	Ctrl+Home
Move to the bottom-right cell on the worksheet, at the intersection of the right-most used column and the bottom-most used row	Ctrl+End
Move down one screen	Page Down
Move up one screen	Page Up
Move one screen to the right	Alt+Page Down
Move one screen to the left	Alt+Page Up
Move to the next sheet in the workbook	Ctrl+Page Down
Move to the previous sheet in the workbook	Ctrl+Page Up
Move to the next pane	F6
Move to the previous pane	Shift+F6
Scroll to display the active cell (after you have scrolled it off the screen)	Ctrl+Backspace

- *Using the* Microsoft *IntelliMouse ® Explorer to navigate*: If you have a Microsoft *IntelliMouse* ® pointing device, you can use it to move around and zoom in on your worksheet or chart (Table 17.2).

Table 17.2 Using a Microsoft *IntelliMouse* ® to navigate a spreadsheet

To:	Do this:
Scroll up or down a few rows at a time	Rotate the wheel forward or back
Pan through a worksheet	Hold down the wheel button and drag the pointer away from the origin mark in the direction you want to scroll
Zoom in or out	Hold down Ctrl, and then rotate the wheel forward or back

Zooming in and out

Work with a zoom setting that you can read easily, but which shows as much text as possible on the screen. To change the zoom setting, click the down arrow beside the Zoom drop-down list on the right of the Standard toolbar and choose one of the options. You can also type in your own zoom factor, such as 85.

To jump to a different location on the worksheet, zoom out, click the new location and then zoom in.

Finding a spreadsheet

If you cannot remember the name or location of a spreadsheet, you can ask the Microsoft *Excel* ® software to search for the spreadsheet by text contained in the spreadsheet.

Steps for the PC

1. Click the Open button on the Standard toolbar.
2. Click the next to last button (Preview button) in the Open dialogue box toolbar. This button displays the contents of a highlighted spreadsheet.
3. Use the Look in drop-down list at the top of the dialogue box to choose the drive you want to search. If you know the folder, choose that folder.
4. To search the contents of all subfolders in that drive, click Commands and Settings (the last button) in the Open dialogue box toolbar and choose Search Subfolders.
5. At the bottom of the dialogue box, fill in the criteria for the search. For example, if you know that the spreadsheet contains the word 'mail', type 'mail' in the Text or Property box.

6 Click Find Now. After a few seconds of searching, Microsoft *Excel*® lists all documents that contain the criteria you set.

7 Select the file you want to open and click Open.

Splitting and freezing panes

To see two distant parts of a worksheet at once, you can split the screen. You can then scroll separately in each pane. You can split the screen vertically or horizontally.

To split the screen into two panes, drag the split box at the top of the vertical scroll bar or the right of the horizontal scroll bar to the desired position. Note that the cursor changes to a split arrow as you drag.

You can freeze row and column headings so you can view them no matter how far down or to the right you scroll.

- To freeze column headings only, click the cell in the first column (A), just below the headings. If your headings take up only one row, this would be cell A2.
- To freeze row headings only, click the cell in the first row (1), just to the right of the headings. If your headings take up only one column, this would be cell B1.
- To freeze both column and row headings, click the cell just below and to the right of the headings. If both headings take up only one row/column, this would be cell B2. Choose Window > Freeze Panes.
- To unfreeze the headings, choose Window > Unfreeze Panes.

To view two workbooks at once you can split the screen. Open both, choose Window > Arrange. Choose a display option (such as Tiled) and click OK. You can also **toggle** between several workbooks by choosing Window and clicking the workbook file. (In Microsoft *Excel*® 2000 you can choose from any open workbook on the Taskbar.)

Printing

How to print a file

1 To see how the worksheet will fit on a sheet of paper, click Print Preview on the Standard toolbar.

2 To print part of a worksheet, drag from one corner to the diagonally opposite corner to select the cells. Then choose File > Print Area > Set Print Area.

3 To format how the page will look, choose File > Page Setup. Here you can set page orientation, scaling, margins, headers and footers, titles, page order, whether or not to print the gridlines you see in the worksheet, and more. Click OK when you are done.

4 Once you have set everything up, click Print on the Standard toolbar or choose Print from Page Setup or Print Preview.

Excel Viewer

With Microsoft *Excel Viewer*®, you can open, view and print Microsoft *Excel*® workbooks, even if you do not have *Excel*® installed; you can also copy data from *Excel Viewer*® to another program. However, you cannot edit data, save a workbook or create a new workbook. This download is available from Microsoft's main site and is free.

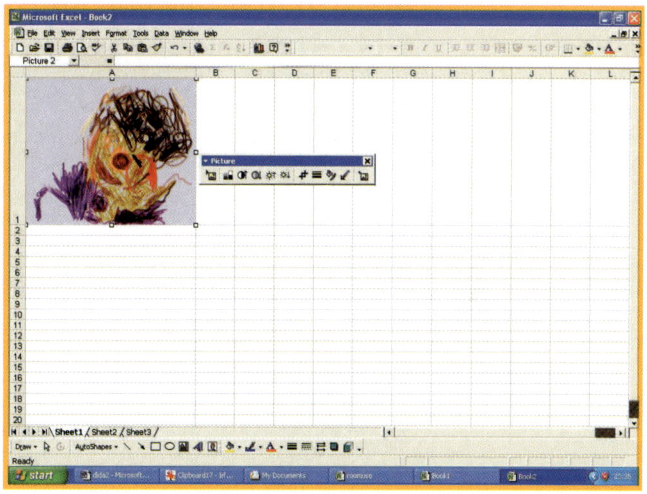

The golden rules for using Microsoft *Excel*® to show data graphically are:

- Keep the charts simple and easy to understand.
- Do not use difficult-to-read text.
- Bear in mind the age of your audience.
- Do not give too much information at once.
- Do not be afraid to incorporate the graphics in the Drawing bar to help make things clearer.
- Remember, there is a simple version of Microsoft *Excel*® in Microsoft *Word*®.

Microsoft *Excel*® software can be used for producing lists of information and it is easy to bring in images, including photos, clips and scanned images, so try to use it creatively. You do not have to use it purely for number crunching. Many people use it to help place items for a poster, or to format a page, using the cells as individual placeholders.

Homework

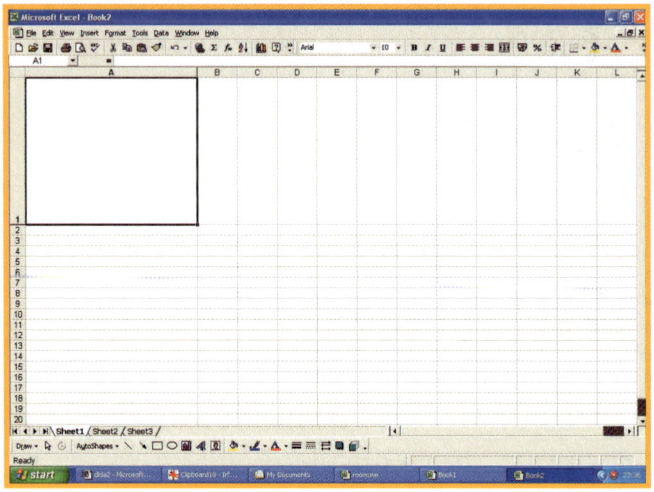

1 List a group of friends and sort the list alphabetically. Format the list using fonts, alignments and colour.

2 Use a spreadsheet application to produce a poster. Increase cell sizes to accommodate images and clip art.

3 Collect some simple data, perhaps the cost of food in a canteen. Record it in a spreadsheet and sort into highest to lowest; produce charts to illustrate the statistical nature of the data. Place the charts into a Microsoft *PowerPoint*® presentation for others to view.

CHAPTER 18

Website software

What you will learn in this chapter

In this chapter you will learn about web-designing software and what software does which job best. You will come across words or jargon, which will be explained, and you will get tips on designing web pages.

In earlier chapters we have looked at paper-based and on-screen publications. This chapter is concerned with the online counterpart – websites. All the rules that influence desktop publishing (DTP) and presentation design should come into play when designing websites, but there is a whole range of other rules to consider.

Before you can even start to design a web page you need to have content. What will your page have on it? You do not need to be precise at this point, but you need some idea. Earlier chapters have mentioned the need for gathering resources; web design is another area where you need to start early. As with DTP work, you may need to collect text from one source and images from somewhere else.

All the information you want to display should be collected together and saved in a single folder. The filing of this material will be discussed later, but having it all in one place to start with is extremely helpful.

Load time

The most important thing to bear in mind is, 'How long will it take for the page to load?' If what you produce takes so long to load that the user clicks off it, it does not matter what else you have done, because nobody will ever see it! This aspect of site design is called 'optimising'. It is the operation of making sure that everything on your page works well together and loads quickly.

Most Internet users will only wait a few seconds for a page to load on their screen. The average wait time is 8 seconds: this means that if your web page takes more than 8 seconds to load, the average user will start to click their mouse and move to another page. One way around this is to have things loading quickly to keep their attention, even though the whole page takes a little longer. Reading this paragraph will have taken more than 8 seconds!

There are a number of websites that offer to check your load times. Most professional sites use some sort of **optimisation software**, and are therefore able to keep their load times very low. Two of the most popular sites in the UK are shown below.

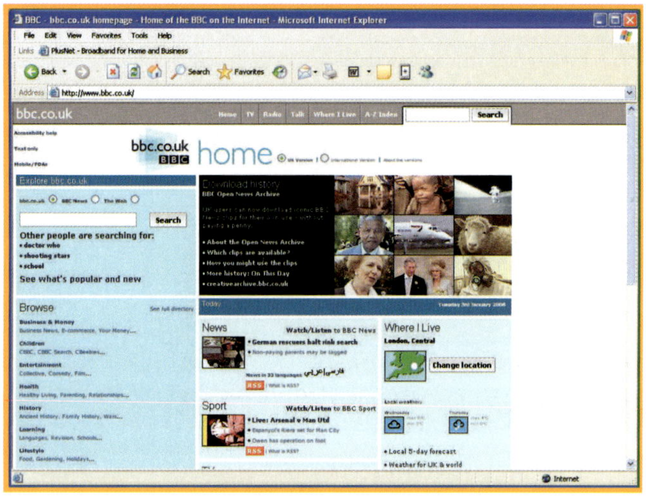

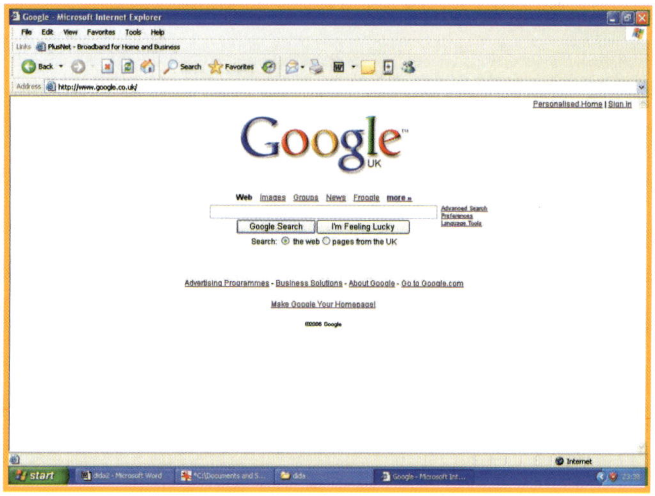

www.google.co.uk takes less than 3 seconds to load.
www.bbc.co.uk takes less than 5 seconds to load.

This time constraint is difficult to plan for, but should be considered at every stage in designing a web page or website. The designer should always have at the back of their mind, 'How long will this take?'

Designing a page

Web pages are very simple to make. They can be generated using a word-processor application or graphics program, and then saved in an appropriate format for viewing through a browser.

There are a number of professional web design applications that you will be using if you want to specialise in this area, Macromedia *Dreamweaver* or Adobe *Go Live* ® software, for example. However, for the purposes of this chapter we will be looking at the general rules of web design and how they can affect the design of a page. More detail on how to use the software is available in the *Multimedia* book.

Many web designers consider layout to be the most important aspect of design, after the load times. When you use a web design application the first thing you are asked is what layout you will be working with. Whatever you design, it must be clear and easy to understand. If you look around on the Internet you will soon find pages that you can understand and others that are confusing and poorly laid out.

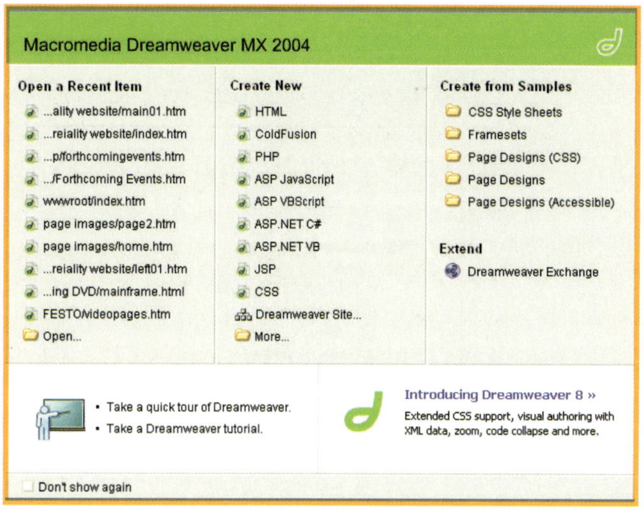

The way most Western people see the world is the way they read – top to bottom, left to right. This also applies to websites: the most important information should be at the top, the left should be for secondary information and the bottom right for the general material.

If you look at newspapers, magazines and web pages there is a common *feel* to the way they look. When a web page is built, the designer usually takes cues from things around them.

- If you want to design a page that carries lots of text, like a newspaper, then you should look at newspapers and similar publications to get a feel for the ways in which they communicate their information.
- If your page is mostly images, then look at catalogues and magazines to see how they work.
- Pages that carry a mixture of text and images are the most difficult to design well. Again, for inspiration, look through magazines and other publications.

Designing your layout should be done on paper. Most designers are pretty good at art – the creative eye! This is not essential, but being able to sketch your ideas really helps.

When you start to transfer the idea to the computer, there are lots of helpful guides and templates that you can use. When you have some idea of layout, you need to get working on the content.

Content

Earlier it was suggested that your content should all be kept in one folder. That is a good start, but now that you are starting to build your page you also need to think about file structures, as the way the site operates can influence the speed at which your pages load.

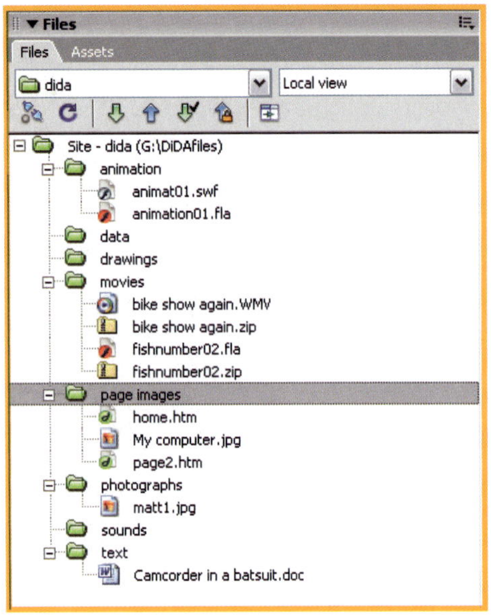

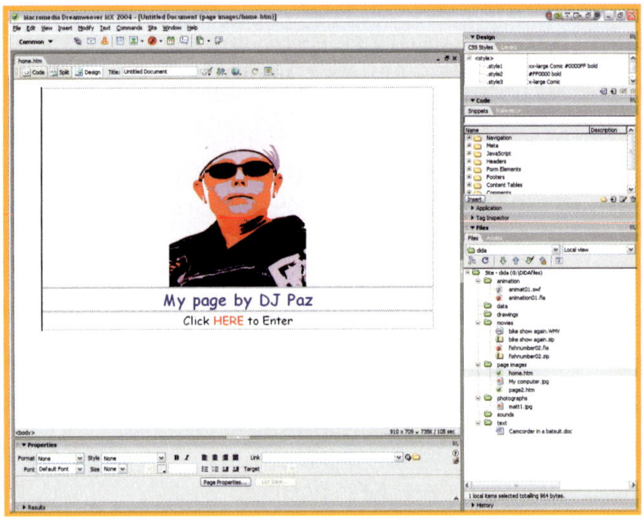

Within your main folder you need two subdirectories:

- Images – where you will keep all the pictures that will be used in your site
- Pages – where all the individual pages will be stored.

Move all your images into the Images folder. The Pages folder will remain empty until you have built some pages.

Every website has a home page – usually called the index. The following exercise shows you how to construct a home page for a DiDA resource, using Macromedia *Dreamweaver MX 2004*. Macromedia *Dreamweaver* can be set up in a number of different ways; we have used the default design view.

The Macromedia *Dreamweaver* desktop is shown opposite.

The main area is where the page will be built.

The right side has a number of palettes containing access to different parts of the application.

The bottom area shows the properties and help areas.

When working with Macromedia *Dreamweaver*, or any other web design application, the software is set up to build a multipage site. You have already set up a simple folder structure and will now be using that as you build your page. The same structure will allow you to build a fully functioning multipage site.

How to build a home page

1 Click on **File > New** – a dialogue box will appear, offering a variety of options.

2 Choose **Basic Page** and **Create**. The blank page will appear as a white background, the top of which holds the page title – as it has not been saved yet, it is 'untitled-1'.

3 Save the blank page in your root folder, not your Pages folder. The index page should be kept separate from the other pages, so that it can be easily accessed for updating.

4 Save your page as Index.htm – the new title should appear on the tab at the top right. You may also notice that the title of the page remains 'untitled document'. This is the title that will be shown by a search engine, so to be a little more professional, it is good practice to change that. It does not have to match the file name, so call it 'DiDA resource'.

5 The **properties inspector** below the page changes as you work, so to make sure that you start off with the correct properties section, move your mouse pointer to the middle of the page and right-click. From the Shortcut menu choose Page Properties . This dialogue box allows you to set various properties for the page. Later you will set properties for elements that will be appearing on the page.

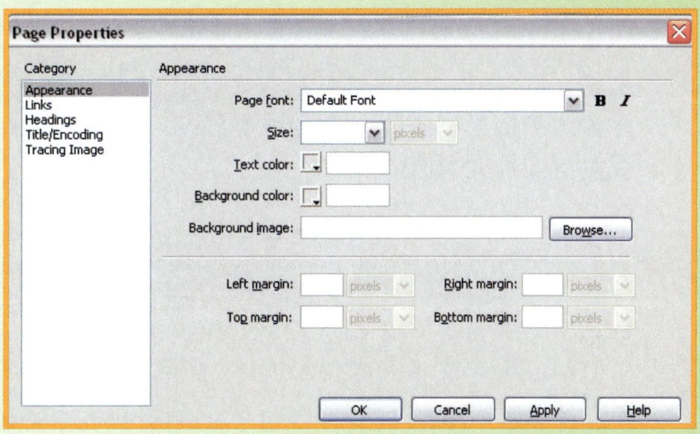

6 First, set the appearance of the page:

Choose a font. You are going to produce a DiDA resource, so you need a professional-looking font. Arial is a good bet – it looks good and is available on most computers.

The size is not important at this point, but colour is. Blue can be much easier to work with, and may also help people who have difficulty reading.Click on the colour picker next to Text color and choose a font colour.

Do the same with Background color: a pale yellow goes well with the blue text.

The rest can stay as they are.

Click Apply and the background should change to the colour you picked. The other settings can be dealt with later, so click OK.

7 Typing straight onto the background is the easiest way to build your page, but it can create difficulties later. So it is much better to enter text into a table. The table can then be formatted or moved easily.

On the toolbar click the Table button; another dialogue box will appear.

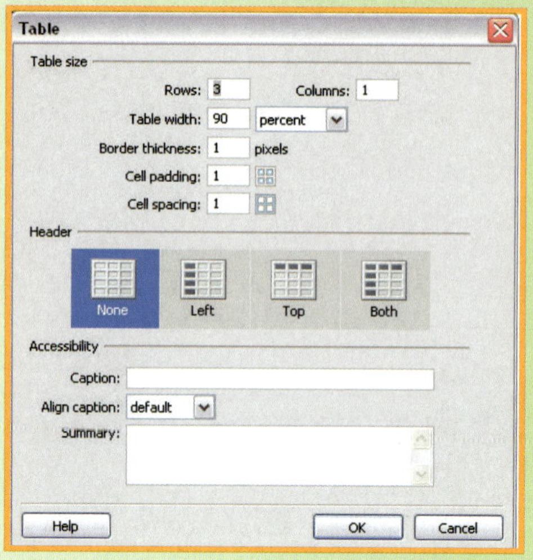

8 This table will contain the title and a short message, so choose two rows and one column.

9 Rather than having the text run right to the edge of the page, if you make the table less than 100% you can have some space down the sides. Choose 85%.

The table should be invisible, so leave the other settings as 0.

10 Macromedia *Dreamweaver* has a number of helpful additions to enable designers to make their pages accessible to all users. Add a summary: 'This is the home page for our DiDA resource'.

11 Click OK. Your table will appear as a dotted boundary at the top of your page. The insertion point will be flashing in the top left cell, aligned left.

12 Click on the border of the cells and the table will be highlighted. The properties inspector will have altered to show settings for the table, rather than the contents of the table.

13 To make the table appear centrally at the top of the page, click in the Align box and choose Centre.

14 It is also a good idea to give your table an identification. In the Table ID box enter 'title block'.

15 You can now start to enter text, directly into the table. Start with a title in the top cell. Then enter some text into the second cell. The properties inspector allows you to format the text as in a word processor, so try out the different options until you have your text looking how you would like it.

16 When you are happy, press F12 to preview your page in a browser. You may have to save the page before it can be previewed. If you resize the browser window, you will see that the text automatically reflows – this is one of the reasons for using a table to place the text. If the text goes straight onto the background it will not reflow so easily. By centring the table you can see that the title remains central, even if the page is resized.

17 Below the table you need to add an image. Click on the image icon on the toolbar and a dialogue box will open up, displaying your folders. Navigate to your Images folder and select an image. Click OK.

18 If your images are straight from a digital camera, or scanned, they may be far too large for a web page. If they are, or even if they just need a bit of tweaking, Macromedia *Dreamweaver* can jump straight into Macromedia *Fireworks* software to edit the image.

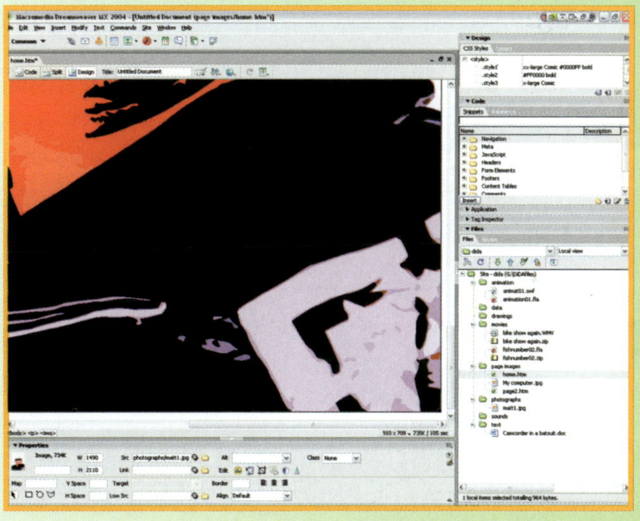

The image that has been brought in to the screenshot opposite is far too large. The property inspector has a button to Edit in Fireworks. Click on the image and then click on the button.

If you do not have this application, you will need to edit it in another graphics package.

Resizing the image in Macromedia *Dreamweaver* will not reduce the file size, so although the image may be smaller, the actual file may still be many megabytes.

19 Macromedia *Fireworks* will open and display your image; you can now edit the image to make it more suitable for use.

An image straight from a digital camera can be enormous, but for use on this page it needs to be approximately 5 cm wide, at 72 dots per inch (**dpi**). After adjusting it in Macromedia *Fireworks*, it is automatically updated in Macromedia *Dreamweaver*. Remember load speed is important, so images need to be small and of a low resolution; 72 dpi is perfect for on-screen images.

20 When you are happy with the size of the image, you can think about positioning it where you want it. As in word-processing packages, an image is seen as a character. It is moved in the same way as a typed letter is moved. Again, it may be best to place it in a table, as this will allow it to be moved more easily.

When it is in place, click on it and go to the property inspector and click in the Alt box. Enter a title or explanation for the image; this will be read by a screen reader for users who do not show images in their browser, or for visually impaired users.

21 To add rows to your existing table, click in the bottom cell and press Tab – as in most other applications, a new row is added.

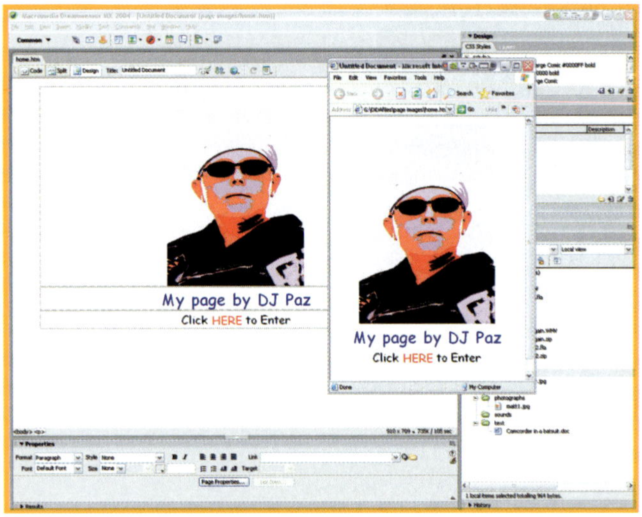

Now it is time to add more information – not much, as this is the home page. You just need to add something about what can be found on the other pages you will be developing at a later date.

As you can see in the image, more text has been added and the format of the text has been altered to make it look more appropriate.

- The list of DiDA units has been made into a bulleted list. This makes it clear that each title is separate, but they are all part of the same qualification.
- The sentence about the following pages has been made bold, to catch the reader's

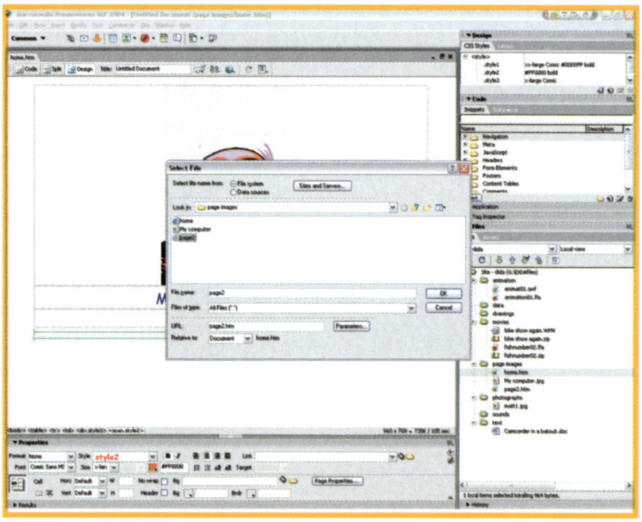

eye: it is important that the reader sees that there are other pages to look at.

- The page links have been entered into their own cell. This involved splitting the cell, using the button on the property inspector, and making four cells in the bottom row.

Press F12, when you have added some detail to your page, and view it as it would be seen over the Internet.

Tip

Before starting to work on a new page, make sure you have saved your home page.

As it now appears there will be at least four more pages to this site, we had better build them!

How to build the other pages

The remaining pages of this website are going to contain only a little content; they can be added to at a later date. They are purely to illustrate how linking works.

1. In Macromedia *Dreamweaver* go to File > New (or Ctrl N) > Basic Page > Create.
2. Save the new page in your Pages folder as 'page 1'.
3. Change the title to 'page one of the DiDA Resource'.
4. Add a table with two rows and four columns.
5. Merge the middle two cells of the top row.
6. Add an image from your Images folder; you may need to edit the image, as with the image on the home page. Remember to add a comment in the Alt box of the property inspector.
7. In the four cells in the second row add the text:

   Home
   Page 2
   Page 3
   Page 4

   As this is page 1, it does not need a link to page 1, but it does need a link back to the home page.
8. Format the page and table to make it all look better than the default settings.

9 Do the same for pages 2, 3 and 4.

The text in the cells must be altered:

Page 2 text:

Home	Page 1	Page 3	Page 4

Page 3 text:

Home	Page 1	Page 2	Page 4

Page 4 text:

Home	Page 1	Page 2	Page 3

10 Make sure all five pages are saved.

Hyperlinking

The ability to hyperlink pages is one of the great advantages of a website over printed materials. To make a section of text link to another element in a website you first need to have all the elements saved, as the software can only link to something that has a saved version.

How to make links from the home page to the other four pages

1 Click and drag on the text 'page 1' in the bottom left cell of the table on the home page.

2 Click on the Browse for file button next to the Link box of the property inspector.

3 This will open a dialogue box showing your 'site files'. Open the Pages folder and click on the page 1.htm file, then click OK.

4 The file name and relative address will appear in the Link box. Below the Link box is a Target box; if you leave this blank and a user clicks on

the link, the home page will be replaced, in the same window, with page 1. This is normally all right, but you may want it to open in a new window. If you do there is a range of options available from this drop-down menu.

5 Make the hyperlinks for the other three pages in exactly the same way.

If the links have been made, the text will be underlined and blue (as the text was blue on this page already, it will not appear to change).

Adding the links to the other pages is a little easier.

Tip

Once you have added links to a webpage, check them regularly and remove or update any that are no longer in use. This will save your readers being frustrated by being led to 'pages not found' pages.

How to add links to other pages

1. Open page 1.htm
2. Click and drag to highlight the text for the home page and click on the Browse for file button. Navigate to the home page and click OK.
3. Click and drag to highlight the text 'page 2'. Then click on the drop-down arrow in the Link box. The available hyperlinks are stored there, from the links you have made so far.
4. Because these are relative links, click on pages/page 2.htm and that will appear in the Link box, but delete the text before page 2.htm, as this page is in the same folder as the page you are linking from.
5. Choose the correct link and then move on to do the page 3 and page 4 links in the same way.
6. Open page 2.htm and add the links to the correct text. All the links you will need are now stored in the Link box, so you will not need to navigate to find the correct files.

7 Do the same for pages 3 and 4.

8 Make sure all your pages are saved – File > Save All (Alt F, shift l).

9 Go to your home page and press F12. Your browser will show the home page, and if you click on the text you have just made into hyperlinks, the pages should change.

10 Check all your links, and if any do not work go back to your page in Macromedia *Dreamweaver* and change the link in the property inspector.

11 The last stage is to add an external hyperlink – this is a link to a page on a website that is not part of the site you have just developed. In this case, the link is to the Edexcel site. On the home page, highlight the text 'Edexcel'.

12 Click in the 'Link' box and type the link: http://www.edexcel.org.uk

13 To ensure that you have the correct link and the text is exactly right, it may be better to open a browser and check the link, by entering it into the address bar. If it is correct, copy and paste it into the Link box. Click on the drop-down arrow in the Target box and select Blank – this will make the browser open a second window to display the new page.

14 Save the page and preview it. The text 'Edexcel' will be underlined and if you click on it a new window will open; if you have access to the Internet it will display the Edexcel home page.

There is a lot more to Macromedia *Dreamweaver* software, some of which you will come across in the *Multimedia* book. But as you now have a simple five-page site, experiment with some of the other tools: add an email link, make the images into hotspots or alter the properties of the tables so that the pages look more interesting.

Homework

1 Using the structure above, produce a full website that gives clear information on the DiDA qualification.

There are a number of DiDA sites available where you may get inspiration; try:

http://dida.edexcel.org.uk/home/

http://www.learn2.co.uk/dida

http://dida.nwlg.org/

2 Develop a structure similar to that above for your e-portfolio. Include an index page and then links to each page that you intend to submit.

3 Set up a stopwatch and time the loading of 10 websites.

Copy and complete the table:

URL	Description	Time to load	Was it worth it?

CHAPTER 19

Word-processing software

What you will learn in this chapter

In this chapter you will learn the basics for using Microsoft *Word*® in DiDA. You will read that Microsoft *Word*® can do a lot more than write letters and booklets. You will be able to format text, draw and create shapes for diagrams.

When we talk of word-processing software we really mean software that is specially designed to write with. Programs such as *WordPad*, Microsoft *Word*® and *Notepad* are all word processors. These programs replaced the typewriter, which relied on accurate typists and did not really allow for mistakes, images or a range of fonts.

Microsoft *Word*® is probably the best-known piece of software in the world, used in millions of homes. It is used in many countries, in the language of each country, and is now so powerful you can do just about anything with it!

You can make a web page in Microsoft *Word*®; you can introduce hyperlink; you can draw, paint and create animated text. You can make multiple-choice questionnaires and create posters, leaflets, flyers, advertisements, letters and books. This book was written in Microsoft *Word*®! It is now so powerful people rarely have any idea of all the things you can do with it.

To summarise, Microsoft *Word*®, can be used for:

- Web pages
- Publications
- Posters
- Flyers
- Postcards
- Producing worksheets
- Writing letters
- Storing web pages
- Drawings
- Diagrams
- Painting
- Sorting lists
- Making graphs
- Creating multiple-choice questionnaires
- Scanning in pictures
- Getting photos from a digital camera
- Simple image editing.

Using Microsoft *Word*®

Simply using the keyboard and the mouse, perhaps for clip art, you can quickly use Microsoft *Word*® for constructing letters, posters and booklets.

Shortcuts

The keyboard can be used for more than just typing. It can speed up what is happening on the screen without having to change hands to use the mouse. This can happen when you use shortcuts. These allow you to press one or two keys to create an action on screen. Shortcuts are shown on the drop-down menus. Some you probably all ready know, like Control V = paste.

Counting words in a document

Click into the document you wish to count the words in, make sure no text is highlighted and choose Tools, then Word Count. Microsoft *Word*® displays the number of words and some other statistics. Highlight text to count the words in the highlighted area, and follow the previous instructions.

Working with graphics

It is possible to do good graphic work in Microsoft *Word*® using the drawing and painting, image manipulation and object manipulation tools. Most of the tools for doing this are found in the Drawing toolbar and the Picture toolbar.

Tip

Inserting a text box makes it easier to insert a graphic file.

Inserting graphics

Graphics can be described as images, art or design work, or text that has or will add value to your text. You can insert several kinds of graphics into a Microsoft *Word*® document: a graphic file, clip art that comes with Microsoft Office®, or AutoShapes that are also a part of Microsoft Office® programs. You can also add graphics images using a scanner or images taken with a digital camera.

To insert a graphic file go to Insert, then Picture, then From file. Find the file and select it. Click Insert.

Tip

Click Import clip to add graphic files to the clip art gallery for easy access.

To insert clip art

1 Choose Insert, then Picture, then Clip Art. Microsoft Office® has a huge bank of clip art which is often not installed as it takes up a lot of memory, so you may be prompted to insert your Office CD-ROM for more clip art. This means the image you are looking for is not installed on your computer or network.

2 Click Insert when you have found the clip art you need.

The important thing you need to know about clip art is that everyone uses it and some clip art images are very common and easily spotted. This does not mean you should never use clip art, but you need to think carefully about the image you use and if you could find a better alternative. Clip art is brilliant for fast picture finding and is copyright-free, but is not always the answer.

AutoShapes

These can be found in the Drawing option. To display the Draw toolbar you may need to go View, then Toolbar, then Drawing. Choose from the list and then choose the shapes you want to use. Click inside your document where you wish to add the shape. You can also drag to set the size once it has been inserted. The Lines options allow you to use a range of tools similar to those found on graphics programs, such as freehand pencils and polygon tools.

To change graphics

See Chapter 17 for more details on changing graphic files.

Formatting

Bulleted lists

A bulleted list is a common method of listing words or sentences. To add bullets you go to Format then Bullets and Numbering. Here you can choose from a range of bullet shapes. Remember to highlight the list you wish to apply bullets to. Deselect the text to see the result.

Format painter

Formatting has to do with the font, font size, font, colour, whether the text is bold, underlined, and so on. If you are likely to use the same formatting several times, you can paint the formatting over new text instead of adding the same colour and font over and over.

Select the text that has the formatting you want and click on Format Painter on the standard toolbar.

Aligning text

Aligning means lining your text up evenly to the right or left of the text block or centering the text. To do this, highlight the text, then click an alignment button from the Formatting toolbar (Align Left, Center, Align Right, Justify). Justified text has a straight margin on both sides. You can align text in advance by clicking on your selected alignment box before you type.

> **Tip**
>
> If you need to format several different sections of text with the same format, double-click the Format Painter button. Choose the text that has the formatting you want, and then select all the sections of text that you want to format. Double-click the Format Painter button again to turn it off.

Line spacing

Sometimes the spaces between lines need to be set wider than normal. To do this you need to highlight the paragraphs you wish to change to new line spacing, then click on Format, then Paragraph and then find the Line spacing box.

Numbering pages

Numbering pages is an important feature, especially if you are producing a long publication. To do this, you must be in Page Layout view.

1 Click the Page Layout button at the bottom left corner of your screen.

2 Select Insert then Page Numbers.

Sometimes you may have a title page and may not want it to display a number, in which case, untick the Show number on first page box.

Styles to format text

Earlier on, in Chapter 6, we mentioned styles. Styles can save you a lot of work if you are working on a long, complex document. Microsoft *Word*® comes with a large number of styles already created for you, but you can easily design your own. You will find styles in word-processing or desktop publishing applications. If you have prepared a house style which defines fonts, colour and alignment, you can set up all this in the style palettes.

Tables

Use tables whenever you want your text to be set up in such a way that it becomes organised, or as an alternative to lists. Tables are very easy to set up and can have either text or graphics placed into them, and text sorted into columns or bulleted lists.

To insert a table

Click on Table from the Standard toolbar. There are two basic methods to create a table. Go to Table, then Insert and add the number of columns and rows you need; or you can draw a table simply by dragging out the table as you move your mouse. All tables can be edited.

Once the table has been drawn you can add rows by clicking Table, then Insert, then Rows Above/Below. To add a row at the very bottom of the table, you can also click in the bottom-right cell and press Tab.

Tip

Always click where you want the new row to appear before you select it. To add columns, type in a value in the column box.

To add columns, follow the same procedure, but click Table then Insert Columns to the Left/Right.

Creating a table for use as a database in Microsoft *Word*®

Insert a table with at least two rows and a number of columns corresponding to your database fields. For a survey these may include name, age, answer to question 1, answer to question 2. So you might want the following columns: Name, Age, Q1, Q2.

In row two, type in your data. Whenever you get to the last column of the last row, press Tab to create a new row.

Viewing your document

As we have already mentioned elsewhere, you should enlarge the page if you can to reduce eye strain. Sometimes, in order to see what your layout looks like, you will need to reduce the page size so you can see the whole page.

You can view your document in four different ways. The buttons at the bottom-left corner of your screen allow you to see your file differently in preset formats.

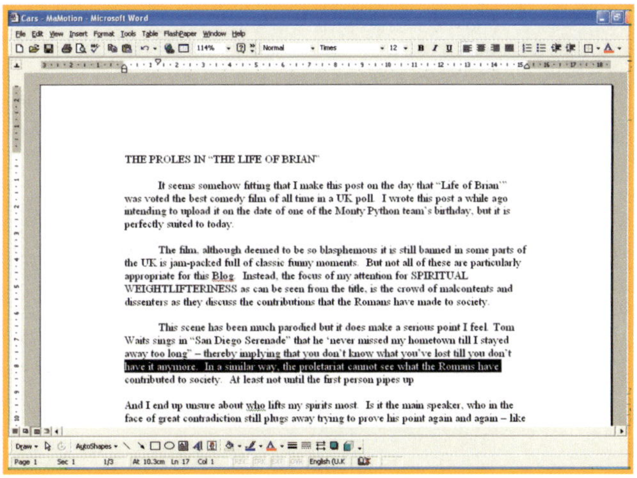

Normal view: shows just plain text, no margins, headers, footers or page numbers. Click the left-most view button at the bottom left of the screen.

Online Layout view: the text is displayed larger than in the Page Layout view. A Document Map to help navigate larger documents can be seen in this view.

Page Layout view: shows the whole document as it will print on paper. It shows everything that will appear as it comes out of the printer.

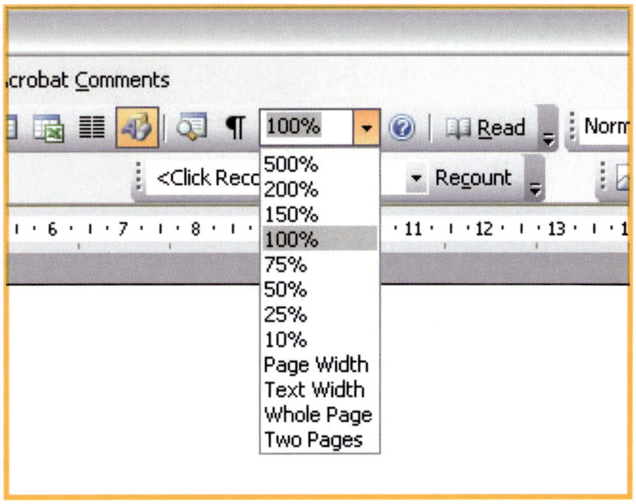

Outline view: helps you when working with a document's structure.

Zooming

You can zoom by going to the View menu and clicking Zoom. This reveals a dialogue box that gives you the option of preset zoom ratios or specifying your own.

Remember, anything you do in Microsoft *Word*® can be placed into other software, such as Microsoft *PowerPoint*® and *Excel*®, and most other software you are likely to come across.

Homework

1. Design a simple text and clip art page for a DiDA project front cover, save it as a web page and then view it through a browser.
2. Using the drawing tools and AutoShapes, draw a plan of your house and garden. Fill with the fill tool.
3. Go to the Internet, find an image and drag it into Microsoft *Word*® using the mouse.

Summative project brief

The final marks you are awarded are based on the SPB. Your teacher will explain what you need to do.

This is the project that the exam board sends to you so that your work can be assesed. This is also the part of the course that you are awarded your grade on, and a focus for all the skills and knowledge you have acquired during your DiDA course!

The brief asks you to solve a problem by using your skills and knowledge to produce a piece of work.

It is recommended that a minimum of 30 hours should be spent working on the brief; your teacher may allow you a little more time. It must be clear to the board that you have done the work yourself and that the work was supervised by a member of staff qualified to do so. The final product must be your own work.

Your SPB (summative project brief) could be built up in one of the following ways:

- Perhaps as a series of mini projects
- Getting information together
- Planning
- Researching
- Making a database
- Market research
- Graphics
- A presentation and a final report.

During this stage you need to save your work carefully and keep a backup. If you lose your work it cannot be marked. If it is saved and is difficult for the examiner to retrieve, you may lose marks. If you fail to complete a part, you will lose marks!

There are details on the e-portfolio elsewhere in this book, and there is information available from the awarding body. Make sure you check anything you are unsure of with your tutor.

Create one main folder for your project. Within this folder you can make separate sub-folders for specific types of work, for example, graphics, databases, research, and so on.

Practice project brief

Below is an example of the kind of SPB the awarding body might set you.

Introduction

Road accidents involving children between the ages of 5 and 15 are too common. Carelessness of children and drivers kills hundreds each year. This is often a result of simply forgetting the Highway Code or the Green Cross Code. Numerous information campaigns have been tried over the years to reduce the number of accidents, and although accident numbers are falling, they are not falling fast enough. Many children would have a greater chance of survival if the drivers of cars observed the speed limits and realised that children may be taught about road safety but can make mistakes. Often drivers do not take this into account.

What can you do?

You are asked to run a **local campaign** that highlights accidents over the last year and danger zones in your area. There are statistics available on road accidents locally, which may help you find out what is contributing to the number of accidents. The campaign should be aimed at both drivers and children. Remember that you may live in an area which tourists come to, or where there are people from different countries who are not familiar with our road systems and warning signs.

Research your subject carefully

- You will need to find out what people's opinions are on this subject.
- You should present your findings to an audience that will range from 5 to 50 years of age.
- If you are informed you should be able to make judgements on what is the best way forward.
- Your work should raise awareness and help to improve the situation.

The work you produce should be in both printed and digital form. It should be easy to read and understand. Each piece of work should show clear evidence of careful research and development.

The items you produce should be:

- A poster advertising a website with the information on it – to be sent to primary and secondary schools.
- A graphic or pictorial tour of your town or village showing likely black spots for accidents – this is to be viewable over the Internet, via standard browser technology. This should be aimed at children.

- A plan of the proposed site, with active buttons linking to further information – either other existing websites or information from a bank of information you have researched.

The whole project must be designed to hold the interest of your target audience and be easy for them to understand. The work should inform and entertain children and be entertaining and fun to use.

The entire project must total less than 15 MB.

When producing these products you should remind yourself of the audience and the purpose. Not everyone taking part in the project has English as a first language, so it will be inappropriate to rely too much on text or speech; make sure you include plenty of graphics and sound.

If you want your audience to enjoy looking at your material, you need to ensure that it works well and that children can understand and operate any interactive material. This means using prototype testing throughout the development of your products and testing them with real users.

If your products are effective, you will have demonstrated your ability to apply your ICT skills in the best possible way.

Before anything else, prepare a work plan, which addresses the questions:

- What information do I need to gather?
- How can it be presented?
- Who will it be presented to?
- Where will it be presented?
- What software would help me?
- How can I store the information?
- What will I need to do first?

Your plan could be produced as a single-sided document, with hyperlinks to various files or folders.

What information do I need?

There is a lot of information out there – how will you find it? (Go back to Chapter 3: Information handling, for advice on this).

You also need to collect information about the needs of the age range you are aiming at, such as reading levels, suitable vocabulary, possible range of languages and appropriate visual information. Remember, your age group is quite varied and will have a broad range of differing reading and writing skills: some may not have English as a first language; some may have learning difficulties; some may be extremely gifted!

You may need to find experts who are planning road layouts and producing safety campaigns across the country. Local newspapers may have covered lots of stories on the subject already. There may also be letters on the subject from members of the public in the local newspapers – this could help you to find out people's opinions on road safety.

You need to gather a variety of multimedia components for use in your product. These components could include video clips, audio clips, text and images. You may be able to use a component in more than one product.

You will need to decide how best to present the information in order to make sure that the audience is able to understand it and be interested enough to want to learn more.

How to present the data

You need to enter the information into an application that will allow you to manipulate it to produce graphic items. You should be able to judge what would work best for each part of your project. Try not to get bogged down with learning too many new skills at this stage. You can probably create databases, make presentations and create and send letters and email spreadsheets. You should also know how to use information from a survey and how to create a sound and valid questionnaire.

At the end you should clearly review what you have done. The information should be presented in such a way that it will keep the attention of the audience you have designed for.

Where to present the graphic products

You will have access to a range of facilities to test your products. Most of it will need to be displayed on a screen. Your website must be viewable with a standard browser.

What software is available?

You need to check with your teacher if you are unsure, but you should have access to Microsoft Office® applications (or similar) and image-manipulation, sound-recording, video-editing, web design, animation and other software.

What's first?

Start by planning what you are going to do and developing a timeline. Build in time to collect components and generate your own resources, as well as manipulating them and combining them for the products.

How can I store the information?

Your tutor will allocate an area on the system for you to save your work, but you will have to set up your own file or folder structure. Remember to keep regular backups.

Hints and tips

Remember, a picture paints a thousand words – use images and video where you can to illustrate a particular idea. Do not rely on everyone reading the text.

Remember that if you do not quickly gain the confidence of your viewer they will go back to something else. You need to convince them that you know what you are talking about. You can use graphics to help get your point across fast.

Do not use fonts that are fiddly; use simple, easy-to-read fonts.

A font designed for online viewing, such as Arial, might be good. Large text is always good! Do not use scripts or complex fonts unless you have a good reason to do so – they are never easy to read.

We all love WordArt in Microsoft *Word*®, but it can be really difficult to read and is better suited to titles or headlines. Children like clear and simple text as many are developing readers and readability is vital. Make it easy for them. Children enjoy bright, fun colours, but if you use them, check that text and background work together.

Get to the point. Do not fill up pages for the sake of it. If the material does not really say anything, get rid of it!

Remember that your audience is bright and may not have much time.

Evaluation

You should evaluate your work throughout the project – how well is your plan working? What did you learn from the prototype? What went wrong and why? Is there anything you could be doing differently?

If you have been keeping a quality log, you should have a record of the feedback you receive while working on the project. You need to use that feedback to inform your choices.

When you have finished your ICT products, review your work. How well does it meet the needs of the audience? Is it fit for the purpose it is intended for? How could it be improved?

Your evaluation could be a written report, but you could also make use of:

- Video clips
- Audio clips
- Presentations.

How to get good marks

- ✓ **Look at the brief regularly and stick to it.**
- ✓ **Remember your aims and stick to them.**
- ✓ **Test, check and evaluate regularly.**
- ✓ **Ask your friends and family to look at what you have done and ask for feedback.**
- ✓ **Check your timeline or plan regularly.**

If you want to lose marks!

- Never refer to your timeline or planning notes.
- Your research is poor or inappropriate.
- Ignore feedback or constructive comments.
- Fail to include elements from each software group.
- Never use your tutors or ask for help when you need it.
- Make your work difficult for others to read or find!
- Have a weak or non-evident evaluation process.

Now is the time to put all your software skills, understanding about project planning, researching, design and evaluation together to complete a substantial project.

The general marking scheme can be found on the Edexcel website by going to www.edexcel.org.uk/quals/gcse/ict/dip/dida/ and looking at the PDF of the specifications. Look for 'Assessing students' work' on the contents page of the PDF.

For Edexcel's DiDA website, on the pages detailing the SPBs, there are 'Mark Alert' icons you can click on to get a checklist of what you need to cover to get good marks.

What should be included in the e-portfolio

The SPB replaces the need for a formal examination and is done over a much longer period of time. Edexcel will set the brief (instructions on how to work through the project), and you will then be assessed on how well you work and the quality of the work you send in.

You are expected to spend the final third of your year on the SPB (approximately 30 hours). Your tutor may guide you during this period, but must not do any of the work for you or tell you exactly what to do.

Your e-portfolio, which is sent to the exam board, must have supporting evidence included.

It should be very easy for anyone to go to any part of your work they wish to view. If it is difficult to navigate your e-portfolio, you may lose marks.

The following is recommended by Edexcel

Your e-portfolio for this year should include the following Edexcel's recommendation will change from year to year to reflect the different SPBs:

- Home page
- Table of contents
- Final products
- Output from the database
- Information leaflet
- Presentation with speaker notes
- Interactive information point
- Letter
- Posters
- Supporting evidence

- Project plan
- References to sources with links where appropriate
- Evidence of database table structure, data entry form, testing and query/search designs
- Questionnaire for survey with evidence of testing
- Spreadsheet including evidence of formulae and testing
- Storyboard for information point
- Review and evaluation of the project outcomes and process including feedback from others and suggestions for improvement.

This web link takes you directly to Edexcel's own site, with a very detailed explanation of the grading system that will be applied to your work when you do it for real:

http://www1.edexcel.org.uk/dida%2Dexemplar/

Good luck!

Analogue – signals which vary continuously for example temperature readings from a sensor.
Application – A piece of software which fulfils a particular, and often specific, task; examples are spreadsheets, word processors, graphics software.
ASCII – American Standard Code for Information Interchange – this is a coding system used to represent characters by using numbers.
Backup File – This is a copy of an original used in case the original is corrupted, damaged or lost.
Bit – The smallest unit of data which represents one character. Bits are only ever either '1' or '0'.
Bitmap – An image which is created in a specialised graphics package, such as Microsoft Paint®. This type of file takes up a lot of memory.
Broadband – This is the term given to fast Internet connections which allow the transportation of large amounts of data quickly.
Browser – A piece of software that is used to access web pages.
CD-ROM – A type of storage medium used to hold large amounts of data. It is used for transportation and archiving large files such as images, presentations and large publications. These files cannot be edited as the user will only have write-read access.
Clickable image – any image which when clicked with a mouse causes some form of action to take place.
Compression – Reducing the size of a large file (often used to reduce the size of large image files).
Co-processor – A microchip that handles a specific task. The fact that it is dedicated to a task means the computer can work on other processes.
Crash – A problem arising when the computer stops working as it should.
Cursor – the pointer that is used to represent the mouse on the screen.
Dialogue box – a window that displays options from which the user can make choices.
Dial-up line – a standard phone line used to connect a computer to the Internet. As the name suggests, a connection has to be made each time you wish to use this.
Digital – a series of pulses in discrete levels.
Directory – a structured area that visually represents the files stored in the computer's memory.
Download – to obtain a file from another computer
DPI – dots per inch – a unit of measurement used to describe the resolution of an image.
DTP – Desk Top Publishing
Email – electronic mail, used to send messages from one computer user to another.
File – information stored on a disk in a particular, predefined format.
Firewall – a means of preventing unwanted intrusion onto a network which is connected to the Internet.
Flatbed scanner – A scanning device that lies flat on a desk – useful for creating digital versions of text documents or images from printed originals.
Folder – An area in which files or other folders are stored.
Font – a style of text.
FTP – File Transfer Protocol – the means by which files are transferred across a network.
GIF – Graphic Interchange Format – a file format used for images.
Graphical user interface (GUI) – The visual representation of the computer system which it easier for users to run applications and carry out computer-related tasks.
Homepage – the main page of any web site.
Host – the main computer to which users are connected.
Hostname – the name which identifies each computer attached to the Internet.
HTML – Hyper Text Markup Language – this used to show

browsers how to portray web pages on the screen.
Hypertext – a means of linking phrases or images on one webpage to other pages or files simply by clicking on them.
Import – to bring data from one document and place it into another document.
Internet – The world's largest network.
Java – A programming language used to create applications that can run within web pages.
JPEG – Joint Photographic Experts Group – a format used for graphics files, particularly photographs.
kB – kilobyte is a unit of data storage
LAN – Local Area Network – a network that is situated within a single site or location.
Line art – images which are not photographs shown in only black and white.
Mail merge – Merging data from a database into a document template to create an individual, automated, personalised document.
Mailing list – list of members of a particular email group.
Memory – the chips where data is stored on a computer.
Menu – list of commands.
Menu bar – the bar on which the menus are displayed.
Modem – A device used to connect a computer to the telephone sytem in order to utilise the internet.
MOV – a file extension used to denote a file created in Quicktime.
MPEG – Moving Pictures **Expert Group** – international standard for video compression. Requires a specialised movie player to be installed on the computer.
Multimedia – a presentation or software that combines a range of media types.
Navigation tools – allows users to find their way around a web site.
Network – a group of computers that are connected in one of a series of ways to form LANs or WANs.
Object–oriented – describes illustrations that are created by mathematical equations.
OCR – Optical Character **Recognition** – used to scan text from a printed document and convert into digital form so that it can be imported into an application such as a word processor.
On-line – any computer that is connected to another computer.
Operating system – the software which controls the tasks on a computer.
Paste – to insert images or text from another source.
Path – a route used to find files stored on a disk.
PDF – Portable Document Format – used to create documents that can be read on any platform of computer – access to a small plug-in is a all that is required to read the document.
Pixel – Picture element – images are made up of pixels.
Plug-in – small programs that are required to run some web-based applications.
Properties – information about an object or file.
Protocols – the rules governing how data is transmitted between devices.
Quicktime – a file extension for movies.
RAM – Random Access Memory. This is the most common type of computer memory and is used to store programs which are being used at the time.
Resolution – this refers to the sharpness of the images that are being shown.
ROM – Read Only Memory – permanent information is stored here.
Scanner – a device used to convert paper-based originals into digital format.
Search engines – web utilities that are used to help a user to find the answer to a query from huge databases of information.
Site – the location of a host.
Spreadsheet – a number-related table which can have calculations applied to it.
SQL – Structured Query Language – the language used by many database systems.

Tags – the formatting codes used in HTML to define the way that content is displayed by a browser.
Taskbar – the bottom of the screen where currently loaded documents and software are displayed.
TIFF – Tag Image File Format – these files are also bitmaps and are their versatility makes them, suitable for transferring files between different applications.
Title bar – the top of a window which contains a name.
Upload – to send a file to another computer.
URL – Uniform Resource Locator – a string of characters that makes up the unique address of a web page.
Web browser – allows you to access HTML documents.
Webpage – the visual representation of HTML codes, text and images.
Word processing – manipulation of text to create documents.
Zipped – compressed version of a program or document.

Index

Index